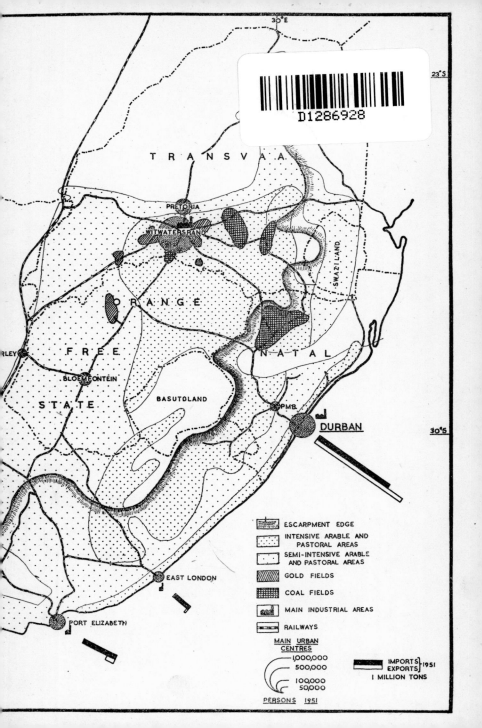

DURBAN

A STUDY IN RACIAL ECOLOGY

Also by Leo Kuper

LIVING IN TOWNS
PASSIVE RESISTANCE IN SOUTHERN AFRICA

DURBAN

A STUDY IN RACIAL ECOLOGY

by

LEO KUPER

HILSTAN WATTS & RONALD DAVIES

with an introduction by

ALAN PATON

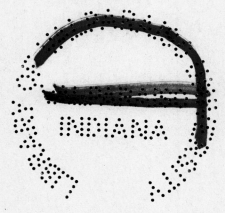

1958

London: JONATHAN CAPE, LTD.

New York: COLUMBIA UNIVERSITY PRESS

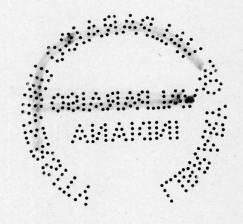

CONTENTS

CONTENTS

FIGURES

TABLES

INTRODUCTION

DURBAN is a fascinating city. It lies on the eastern coast of South Africa, and while its vegetation is as luxuriant as any of the sea-ports to the north, it is spared their oppressive heat. The coastal flats rise relatively sharply to that fine line of hills known as the Berea, with seaward-facing slopes densely covered with splendid trees, among which the early settlers built their homes. They also imported brilliant creepers and trees from other countries, notably the blue jacaranda, the scarlet flamboyant, the orange bignonia venuta, and bougainvillias of many hues.

The character of the city is changing, and its colourful trees are yielding place, on the coastal flats, to tall and modern buildings, on the Berea, to big blocks of apartments. The population, which was 60,000 when I was a boy at school, now exceeds half a million souls, and it is expected to reach the million in the 'seventies. This population is colourful itself; in this year, 1957, it is fairly equally divided amongst the Europeans (whites), Africans (the original natives), and the Indians (most of whom are the descendants of Indians brought here as plantation labourers from 1860 onwards). The city also contains a small number of Coloured people, of the group that is so numerous in the Western Province of the Cape.

There is no need for me to explain what happens when a multi-racial city of 60,000 people becomes a city of half a million. It is fairly easy, and not unnatural, for the different racial groups in a small city to keep more or less to themselves. But as the city of Durban expanded, growing groups encircled and by-passed other groups that had once been on the outskirts, while those groups which lived on the coastal flats tended to penetrate into the areas of the Berea. Poor non-white people had already built houses on the relatively less attractive inland slopes behind the Berea, but as the richer group expanded, it encircled and penetrated these non-white areas.

Elsewhere such matters might have been left to economic forces to settle, but not in South Africa. Here the majority of the European people wished to reside in separate residential areas set apart by law. The European group in Durban was no exception, and in particular they resented the presence on the Berea of Indian people who had 'penetrated' the area. Though in the main politically opposed to the Afrikaner Nationalist Party Government, they welcomed the Government's policies of residential separation as set out in the Group Areas Act of 1950, for they themselves had tried, first in the 'twenties, and later in the 'forties, to achieve the same; what is more, Professor Kuper shows that more than half a century ago the Durban local authority was gravely concerned about the presence of Indians and Africans in and near white residential areas, and was later to be still more concerned about the growing success of Indian business men in the central portion of the city. There is a strong anti-Indian feeling among the white people of the city.

The Group Areas Act aims at the residential zoning of every town and city, so that the goal of complete racial separation can be achieved. The all-white Durban City Council appointed a Technical Sub-Committee to replan the city, and this Sub-Committee took as its guiding axiom the proposition that contact between races in residential areas leads to conflict. It even regarded as 'most objectionable' the large-scale movement of pedestrians of one race through the area of another. It decided to make use of natural boundaries such as 'rivers, steep valleys, cliffs and hill-tops' to effect as complete a racial separation as possible.

In November 1951 the Technical Sub-Committee produced far-reaching plans for the racial zoning of Durban. These plans required the displacement of 70,000 Indians, 8,500 Coloured people, the majority of the Africans, and 12,000 white people. White areas would have gained 3,000 acres at the expense of Indians, valued at £6,000,000.

But white opposition to these plans was too strong. In August 1952 the Durban City Council adopted new plans, whereby only 3,100 white people would be displaced, 55,000 Indians, and 80,000 Africans.

This piece of research, *Durban: A Study in Racial Ecology*, provides a scholar's background to the situation brought about by the application of the Group Areas Act to Durban. It is the joint work of Professor Leo Kuper, Professor of Sociology at the University of Natal, Mr Hilstan Watts, and Mr Ronald Davies. No one is better fitted than Professor Kuper to guide such a study, for he combines the objectivity of the scholar with a warm-hearted feeling for the city and its people.

The authors have given a careful description of the city as it is, racially and topographically, and have indicated the lines which the final proclamations will almost certainly follow. Even those who are strangers to Durban and South Africa will be able to grasp the drastic nature of the proposals, and to realize the vast scope and intention of the Group Areas Act.

But the authors have also permitted themselves some observations on the new situation that will be brought about. In present-day South Africa there is a strong tendency to regard as 'impartial' only those studies which abstain rigorously from any criticism of our present society. It would be quite impossible for the authors of this study to have consented to any abstention on these grounds; nor have they done so. But at the same time they have tried to make it possible for the reader to form his own opinions.

The authors quote in their conclusion the words of

Dr Ebenezer Donges, the Minister of the Interior and architect of the Group Areas Act—

'I also want to say this, that no policy which is not based on justice, has any prospect of success.'

May I give my own conclusion that in that case the Group Areas Act has no prospect of any success at all? It may succeed up to the point in displacing hundreds of thousands of people, and in reducing racial contacts to a minimum. But in driving to its goal the Government appears to be so indifferent to the just claims of persons, so careless of their losses and sufferings, so arrogant in its destruction of their rights, that far from achieving harmony by separation, it is creating the very disharmony that it fears.

'Harmony through separation.' What a fantastic ideal! The very words kill each other, and the phrase presupposes a physical means to a spiritual goal. But here in Professor Kuper's book, the reader may study the colossal steps that one city is taking in a journey that will be meaningless tomorrow.

ALAN PATON

PREFACE

THIS is a study of the racial zoning of the City of Durban. It deals with the present residential distribution of the races, and the plans for their redistribution under a system of compulsory segregation. It is a study, then, in race relations and in planned ecological change, but limited to the residential field, since the present plans for the racial zoning of Durban relate only to residential living. A further limitation is that the major emphasis is placed on the position of the European and Indian groups. This is not from any desire to minimize the importance of the problems which face the African and Coloured peoples of Durban. But Indians and Europeans are the main competitors for the land of Durban, and the problems of compulsory segregation between them are most acute.

We are greatly indebted to the Department of Education, Arts and Science (National Council for Social Research) for a subsidy of £1,600, and to the Director of Census for extracting and tabulating data from the 1951 Union Census for our use. We also wish to acknowledge warmly the very valuable help we received from Dr H. C. Brookfield and Mrs A. Tatham during the early stages of the work and particularly in the preparation of our basic map of Durban. Their knowledge of Durban, and the technical skills they applied as geographers, provided a sound basis for the study, and eased our work appreciably.

We have received help in this study from many different sources. We would especially like to express our thanks to Dr Hilda Kuper, Professor J. D. Krige, Dr C. J. Jooste, Mr S. E. Cruise, Dr S. Cooppan and Mr C. A. Woods, all of the University of Natal, to Mr Alan Paton and Mr P. M.

Brown, to Professor Ed. de S. Brunner of Columbia University, and Professor O. D. Duncan of the University of Chicago, and to Mr W. L. Howes, Town Clerk of the City of Durban, for their comments on the manuscript; to Miss Margo Phillips for her invaluable help as a research assistant, and to Miss Beth Meikle for typing the manuscript. We also wish to acknowledge criticism received from the National Council for Social Research, and Professor S. Pauw of the University of South Africa, as well as assistance from officials of the Durban Municipality and from Mr P. R. Pather of the Natal Indian Organization.

The manuscript was finally revised at the University of Manchester while Leo Kuper held the position of Honorary Research Fellow, and we would like to express our appreciation to the University.

The conclusions reached, and opinions expressed, are our own, and are not to be regarded as those of the Department of Education, Arts and Science.

DURBAN–*August 1957*.　　　　MANCHESTER–*April 1958*.

DURBAN

A STUDY IN RACIAL ECOLOGY

CHAPTER I

RACE CONTACT: CONFLICT OR CO-OPERATION?

TWO opposite theories are held in regard to the consequences of contact between races. One theory is that contact breeds friction. The customs of people of different races are considered to be incompatible, and harmonious relations can therefore be secured only by reducing points of contact to the minimum. This was the theory advanced by the Government of South Africa when it introduced legislation to provide machinery for the segregation of the races.[1] It is also the basis for the replanning of the City of Durban.

The second theory asserts that contact promotes harmony. Common interests are believed to develop from shared experiences and to provide a basis for co-operation. This theory is applied in race relations, more particularly in the United States of America, and generally in Town Planning to build communities and to reduce class antagonisms. So as to increase the range of contact, members of different groups are brought together formally or informally, in contrived situations or in the routine of day-to-day living.

Neither of these theories is adequate in the form in which we have stated them. Clearly, sometimes conflict, at other

---

[1] The Minister of the Interior explained, when introducing the second reading of the Group Areas Bill, that 'points of contact inevitably produce friction and friction generates heat which may lead to a conflagration. It is our duty therefore to reduce these points of contact to the absolute minimum which public opinion is prepared to accept. The paramountcy of the white man and of western civilization in South Africa must be ensured in the interests of the material, cultural and spiritual development of all races.' Hansard, *House of Assembly Debates* (vols. 70–3, 29th May 1950, p. 7453).

times co-operation, develops from the contact of races. The problem is to discover the conditions which produce one or other result. Current research has shown the relevance of such conditions as the level of contact, that is to say, whether the parties meet as equals, or as superiors and inferiors. Reactions will also vary with the type of contact—intimate, as in children's play groups; or relatively impersonal, as in a large-scale business organization. The source of contact, that is to say, the way in which the contact arises—a contrived and possibly self-conscious contact as compared with a spontaneous matter-of-fact contact—may be expected to affect the result. Important, too, is the context or framework of contact—for example, whether there are official policies which govern the contact, and impose or forbid discrimination—and the characteristics of the parties to the contact— their attitudes, embodying interpretations of past experience, their feelings of security or insecurity, the extent to which they share a common purpose, and their material interests, real or fancied.[1]

Precise statements cannot be made at the present time as to the results of contact under different conditions. Indeed, this may never be possible, because of the complexity of the factors involved. Clearly action cannot wait on research. Both theories of contact are directed towards action, and administrators proceed on the assumption that the theory they apply is, in fact, valid. Belief in the validity of the theory is indeed a further condition shaping the final result.

The work carried out by administrators may be regarded as providing raw experimental data for research into the problems of race contact. It is from this point of view that we are approaching the plans of the Corporation of Durban

[1] For a full discussion of relevant factors see Robin M. Williams, *The Reduction of Intergroup Tensions* (New York, Social Science Research Council, pp. 61–77). See also Deutsch and Collins, *Interracial Housing* (University of Minnesota Press, 1951, pp. 124–9), and Wilner, Walkley and Cook, *Human Relations in Interracial Housing* (University of Minnesota Press, 1955, pp. 155–61).

for total residential segregation, or the complete avoidance of contact, as neighbours, between people of different race. These plans are based on the recommendations of a Technical Sub-Committee of the City Council, appointed on the 20th November 1950, and initially provided for a radial pattern of development into segregated residential ribs or spokes, extending, in the shape of a fan, from the industrial and central business belt. Since the population of Durban consists, in almost equal proportions, of Europeans, Indians and Africans,[1] and since the present residential distribution of the races is partly concentric, partly radial, and partly mixed, the carrying out of the plans involves a large resettlement of residents.

The results of the City Council's race zoning will require study over a long period of years. For this purpose we need information about Durban at a 'zero' point of change, at a time, that is, immediately before the publication of the replanning proposals and the regrouping of the races. The 1951 Union Government Census is a convenient starting point. It gives information as to the racial composition of Durban, the demography of each of the races, and their spatial distribution.[2] The main object of our inquiry is the analysis of this information, to provide a basis for the study of the consequences of Durban's experiment in total segregation as they unfold over the years. A subsidiary object is to trace the implications of the experiment, and to suggest lines of research which may throw light on the conditions under which contact or avoidance of contact between races promotes harmony or conflict.

★

[1] We have followed the Union Census in our use of the term 'European' for the white population. The 'Asiatic' population in Durban is almost entirely Indian, and we therefore prefer this term, in discussing Durban, to the census description 'Asiatic'. Since many people regard the official designation of 'Native' as derogatory, we have substituted the term 'African' wherever possible. By 'race' we mean any group defined as a racial group in South Africa.

[2] By special arrangement with the Director of Census, we were given the Census data for Durban on the basis of a breakdown of the City into 36 areas.

The present pattern of residence in Durban is based on the segregation of the races. This was imperfectly achieved in the past, and is now to be perfected under the City's new plans. The legislative trend in the Province of Natal has been from voluntary to compulsory segregation. It is linked with developments in Non-European policies throughout the Union of South Africa and must be set in this wider background.

The application of a policy of compulsory segregation to the African (Native) population was easily solved. Territorial segregation of Africans has deep historical roots in South Africa. Already during the nineteenth century, separate areas were set aside for them in the four provinces. After the union of the provinces, the Government passed the Natives Land Act, No. 27 of 1913, which was designed to enforce territorial segregation in the rural areas. Similar control was extended to the urban areas by the Natives (Urban Areas) Act, No. 21 of 1923, which provided machinery for segregation in locations and villages within the towns. An amendment in 1937 virtually debarred Africans from acquiring property from other races in cities and townships, thus 'pegging' the *status quo*. Later, the Governor-General was given power to declare that all Africans in the urban area should reside in a separate village, location or hostel, domestic servants, among others, being exempted from this provision.[1] The Group Areas Act of 1950, as amended by Act No. 29 of 1956, merely completes the legislative process for compulsory segregation of Africans.

The position in relation to the Indians is far more complex. There is a maze of laws, judicial decisions, and commission reports, which gives the impression of a continuous conflict between Europeans and Indians for land and trade, and of European solutions by way of segregation and repatriation.

[1] K. Kirkwood, *The Group Areas Act* (South African Institute of Race Relations, Johannesburg), and E. Hellman, 'Urban Areas', in *Handbook on Race Relations in South Africa* (Oxford University Press, 1949, pp. 230–8).

It is an incomplete picture. Commissions are not appointed to investigate the harmonious working of society; historians are more readily attracted to chronicles of conflict than of co-operation. Hence the documentary evidence is largely of conflict, and it is in these terms, too, that Europeans generally define their relations with Indians. Yet co-operation was the dominant factor. The Indian community in South Africa has its origin in the indentured labour which was introduced by the province of Natal between 1860 and 1911, mainly for the development of the sugar, tea and wattle plantations, the railways and mines. When immigration ceased for a few years after 1866, the sugar industry suffered so seriously that, on further representations and appeals from Natal, immigration was resumed in 1874 and continued without material interruption until 1911. The sugar planters had become dependent on Indian labour: African labour was unreliable, and practically unobtainable.[1]

This indentured labour, recruited mainly from the agricultural labouring classes, came in two streams, one from Madras (largely Tamil- and Telugu-speaking) and one from Upper India (mainly Hindi-speaking). The majority settled in Natal on the expiry of their indentures. They were followed by traders, mostly Muslim from the Bombay Presidency, at first to supply the wants of the indentured labourers, but later extending their dealings to other groups and other provinces.

Prior to Union, the four provinces reacted in very different ways to Indian immigration. In the Orange Free State Asiatics could neither trade nor own land, in terms of a law of 1891, and they were practically debarred from entry or residence. The Orange Free State may have an Indian

---

[1] Our account of the history of Indian settlement and legislation is based on the *Report of the Asiatic Inquiry Commission*, U.G. 4/1921; M. Webb, 'Indian Land Legislation' in *Handbook on Race Relations in South Africa*, previously cited; and G. H. Calpin, *Indians in South Africa* (Pietermaritzburg, Shuter and Shooter, 1949).

problem, in common with the Union as a whole. It has virtually no Indians.

In the Transvaal the Government immediately responded to the first incursion of Indians by passing Law No. 3 of 1885, which provided that Asiatics could own fixed property only in streets, wards and locations assigned to them for their residence. It sought, unsuccessfully, to extend these powers for the segregation of ownership and residence, to trading. The right to mine minerals was reserved to Europeans, and the Gold Law of 1908 provided that, save in Native Locations, no rights in proclaimed land (i.e. the mining areas), might be acquired by a coloured person, whether as owner, lessee or occupier. However, the statutory powers of the Government were not rigidly enforced; there were disputes as to their interpretation, and some legal means for the acquisition of property rights. The result was that, prior to Union, power to compel segregation of ownership, residence and trade in the Transvaal was not complete, and Indians had acquired vested rights to fixed property.

In the Cape Colony the approach was entirely permissive. There, Indians enjoyed the parliamentary and municipal franchise, in contrast to the Orange Free State and the Transvaal, and also unrestricted rights to trade and own land. This was the position initially in the Province of Natal. Indeed, in Natal, inducements were offered to indentured Indians, so as to secure their continued residence in the Colony. A Natal law of 1859, repealed in 1891, provided that Crown lands could be allocated to those immigrants who, on expiry of their indentures, elected to remain in the country, and by 1885, whether by grants or purchase or lease, about 2,000 Indians were in occupation of land, as market gardeners or small farmers, within two miles of the boundaries of Durban.[1]

When the number of 'free' Indians began to increase, Europeans in Natal became agitated. Already, in 1885, the

---

[1] Webb, 'Indian Land Legislation,' op. cit., p. 206.

Natal Government appointed the Wragg Commission to consider whether the system of indentured Indian immigration should continue. This Commission reported that most white colonists felt that the Indian immigrant must remain under indenture during the whole period of his residence within the Colony; they were strongly opposed to the presence of the free Indian as a rival and competitor, either in agriculture or commerce. Some angrily demanded that the introduction of Indian immigrants should forthwith cease, and that the 'Kaffirs' resident in the Colony be forced to work. Others were prepared to accept the present system, provided the status of the free Indian was reduced to a lower level by a deprivation of rights.[1]

Already, the attitudes of the English settlers of Natal and of the burghers of the Transvaal were beginning to converge, and, in fact, the Maritzburg Chamber of Commerce petitioned the Legislative Council of Natal to pass a law for the compulsory segregation of Asiatics, similar to that in the Transvaal. There was, however, the fundamental difference that the sugar industry of Natal needed Indian labour. Partly for this reason, and partly because of the influence of the Imperial Government, the attitudes of the English settlers were not fully translated into official policy.

Some major steps were, however, taken. The Disfranchisement Act of 1896 abolished the parliamentary vote of Indians, though retaining on the general roll Indians already registered—a category now almost extinct. To discourage Indian settlement in Natal, a tax was imposed on indentured Indians who elected to remain after expiry of their indentures; and there were restrictions on free, but not indentured, Indian immigration. Control over Indian trade was secured by the appointment of licensing officers, with discretion to issue or refuse licences. The position in Natal, therefore, was that, prior to Union, the white settlers could not enforce segregation in ownership or residence, though

[1] *Report of the Asiatic Inquiry Commission*, p. 41.

they could restrict Indian trade indirectly through the discretionary powers of the licensing officers.

When the Union was formed the '*hereditas damnosa*'[1] of the Asiatic question was bequeathed to the Union Government. It immediately sought to limit the Indian population by the restriction of immigration and the encouragement of repatriation. The South African Government has never been in a position to accede to the demands of Europeans for compulsory repatriation, and assisted repatriation schemes, under more attractive conditions as the years passed, were not sufficiently effective to reduce materially the Indian population of the Union.[2]

During the period of assisted repatriation the Union Government did little to compel segregation. Some of the 'loopholes' in the old Transvaal law of 1885 were closed. In 1924 and again in 1925 the Government proposed legislation conferring powers for compulsory segregation. However, it did not proceed with this legislation, but persevered further with assisted repatriation, in terms of an agreement with the Indian Government, which included an undertaking to 'uplift' the Indian residue which would remain permanently resident in South Africa.[3] When it became clear that the residue would be the bulk of the Indian population, and under continued pressure of European agitation against the acquisition and occupation of property by Indians in European areas, the Government appointed a number of commissions. It adopted temporary

[1] Phrase used by the *Asiatic Land Tenure Laws Amendments Committee and the Land Tenure Act Amendments Committee*, in Government report U.G. 49/1950, and indicative of the Committee's attitude.

[2] From 1915 to 1919 the number of Indians in Natal who made use of assisted repatriation more than counterbalanced the natural increase. Between 1920 and 1927, under a new scheme of repatriation, 11,487 Indians returned to India. With still more attractive repatriation facilities, 17,542 Indians, mostly from Natal, left the Union between the years 1927 to 1940.—Wives and children of South African Indians were allowed to enter the Union and, from 1927 to 1940, 2,212 availed themselves of this concession.—(*Report of the First Indian 'Penetration' Commission*, U.G. No. 39/1941, para. 15.)

[3] See Webb, 'Indian Land Legislation', op. cit.; Calpin gives a full account of the history of the legislation in *Indians in South Africa*.

expedients in the way of 'Pegging' Acts, designed to maintain the existing distribution of property between Europeans and Indians in the Transvaal and in Durban. These were followed, in 1946, by the Asiatic Land Tenure and Indian Representation Act, providing for the demarcation of areas, outside of which no Asiatic might acquire from a Non-Asiatic the ownership or residential occupation of land, save under permit. By way of compensation, Indians were offered limited political representation on a communal basis: this offer they rejected and it was subsequently withdrawn.

The Asiatic Land Tenure Act was the first general provision made for compulsory segregation throughout Natal.[1] It did not, however, deprive the Indians of their right to retain fixed property acquired over eighty years of settlement. This final power was assumed under the Group Areas Act and the Group Areas Development Act. There is now no limitation whatever on the powers of the Government to rearrange areas of Indian residence, ownership and trade. Legally, from the point of view of spatial distribution, it is as if the Indians were entering the Union for the first time. In practice, their established settlements seriously impede the establishment of Group Areas. This is especially so in the City of Durban.

The unwillingness of the provinces of the Union to share the Indian population, reflected in the legal restrictions against inter-provincial movement, has resulted in the concentration of Indians in the province of Natal. According to the 1951 Census, there are 366,664 Asiatics (mostly Indians) in the Union or 2·9 per cent of the total population. The Orange Free State has 13 Asiatics; the Cape, 17,818 or 0·4 of 1 per cent of the Cape population; the Transvaal, 49,342 or 1 per cent of its total, while Natal has 299,491 Asiatics or 12·4 per cent. Of the total Asiatic population,

[1] Transvaal Law No. 3 of 1885 applied in the Northern Districts of Natal, but not elsewhere in Natal.

43·8 per cent lives in Durban and suburbs adjacent to the municipal boundaries.

This concentration, and the impotence to compel total segregation in the past, explain the role of Natal, and more particularly of the City of Durban, as a driving force behind the legislation which culminated in the Group Areas Act. If the indentured labourers had returned to India on completing their indentures, or even remained to work as labourers in the industries of Natal, there would have been little complaint, but it was a continuous source of conflict that this kind of labour should compete freely with Europeans for the land, trade and wealth of Natal. The main target for European resentment was, however, the more serious competition of the so-called 'passenger' Indians, who arrived, not to labour under indenture, but to trade as free persons.

In Durban the early settlement of Africans was not controlled. The Mayor's Minute of 1887 reports a public meeting which discussed assaults and other crimes by Africans and asked that locations be established at a convenient distance from the town. Most Africans lived in shacks and hovels, and were not residentially segregated. The only planned accommodation consisted of barracks for male labourers, and the numbers of these barracks, established by the City Council and by private enterprise, rapidly increased. The general policy was to achieve segregation without compulsion by attracting the population to the segregated facilities. It is only in 1916 that the Mayor refers to the framing of by-laws under which penalties can be enforced against Africans who live in unauthorized places and against the proprietors who allow them to live there.[1]

Municipal Housing for African families was a later

---

[1] 'Native Location By-Laws for the Borough of Durban,' *Natal Provincial Gazette*, 15th June 1916, p. 436.

development. In 1912, the Mayor's Minute mentions the opening of a Women's Hostel, and in 1927, for the first time, the development of a village or location. From then onwards the City Council went ahead with the building of family homes in segregated areas. This development has not kept pace with rapid urbanization, and most African families are settled in shack dwellings, segregated from the European population.[1]

The present general pattern of African residential living is thus, for male labourers, compounds or barracks in the commercial and industrial areas; for families, municipal locations and shack settlements (authorized and unauthorized) on the outskirts of the city; and for domestic workers, men and women, the back-yards of European, and to a small extent Indian, homes. Ownership by Africans of immovable property in Durban is negligible. According to an estimate by the Technical Sub-Committee on Race Zoning,[2] Africans owned property to a value of £112,180 covering 105 acres (less than 0·1 of 1 per cent of the value of property in Durban and about 0·25 of 1 per cent of its area). Clearly the Group Areas Act may affect the distribution of the African population: segregation from Europeans both in terms of ownership and occupation—apart from domestic servants—is however relatively complete at the present time.

The Coloureds are a small proportion of the population of Durban (under 4 per cent). They still enjoy the municipal franchise and a restricted parliamentary franchise. The Group Areas Act extends to the Coloureds the principle of compulsory segregation. Prior to that date, Coloureds were free to own and occupy property where they pleased, save in areas specifically reserved to Europeans, and their segregation was not a local issue.

In the case of the Indians, however, the City Council

---

[1] For a detailed account of African Housing in Durban, see *The Durban Housing Survey* (University of Natal Press, 1952), chapter XI.

[2] *Race Zoning Proposals*, Part III of First Report, dated 26th November 1951, p. 173.

was preoccupied with the problem of their segregation from the earliest days. In 1871, the Mayor in his Minute reports complaints about the building of 'Coolie dwelling houses' in the town. Two years later he comments on the probably disastrous effects of selling or leasing properties in the town to Indians, and refers to the appointment of a committee to select suitable sites for their location. The following year he mentions 'the further erection and habitation of Coolie shops in our very midst, with their belongings of dirt and other objectionable things, which to be realized, can be seen at present at the West End and other parts of the town'. In 1875, he begins to feel that 'legislation will doubtless have to be resorted to, to prevent these people thus locating themselves in our very midst, their habits and customs being, as is well known, so totally at variance with and repugnant to those of Europeans'. The Superintendent of the Borough Police, in 1889, reports on the increasing number of Indian retail stores in the town, and recommends that no licences be given to Indians for any building in the three main streets. In 1897, the Council acquires the power to refuse licences to applicants, and in 1903 the Mayor urges that prompt steps be taken to introduce legislation for the registration of Asiatics in Durban and for the laying out of bazaars or locations, and that no new licences of any description should be issued to Asiatics except for premises in such locations. It was to be almost fifty years before the Government made the requested legislative provision.

Lacking the necessary powers, the City Council tried to bring about segregation by means short of compulsion. Control over trading licences was sufficiently effective to ensure that Indian trading areas today are largely separate from European. As for residential segregation, whatever barrack accommodation and housing the Council provided was on a segregated basis. It could not control private housing in this way. However, an Ordinance in 1922 (No. 14) gave the Council power, when selling or leasing land, to reserve occupation or ownership for a particular racial group. This power was invariably used to establish racially exclusive suburbs for Europeans, but not for Indians, who persistently refused to accept segregatory restrictions.[1] Since at about the same time Indians lost the municipal franchise, they were little able to influence Council policies away from segregation.

The provision of municipal housing for Indians was a relatively late development, and inadequate for their needs.[2] One can only speculate what the pattern of Indian settlement might have been if the Council had assumed fuller responsibility at an earlier date, and if it had been prepared to develop Indian areas as adequately as European areas. As it was, Indians had to rely largely on their own resources. They settled in the low-lying areas of the city, the relatively swampy areas, and outside the boundaries. Most of their housing, of low standard, was in the peri-urban areas. When, in 1932, these were incorporated into the Borough, the Indian population of the city was more than trebled, and the housing problem greatly magnified.

In the process of establishing themselves, Indians acquired considerable holdings of immovable property in the city. The Technical Sub-Committee on Race Zoning estimated the value of property owned by them in 1950–1 as £24,541,060, and its extent as 10,323 acres[3] (or 13·7 per cent of the total value of property in the city, and 26·0 per cent of its acreage). Most of this land is in the predominantly

---

[1] *Report of the First Indian 'Penetration' Commission*, op. cit., para 23. Some private townships also had conditions in the title deeds, restricting ownership and occupation to Europeans.

[2] Early provision of accommodation for Indians was of very low standard. The Protector of Indian Immigrants, in 1884, described the municipal barracks as 'neither huts nor houses but dens quite unfit for humanity to live in', and accommodation provided by other European employers as 'very inferior ... the huts being contracted in size and immensely overcrowded'. The first Indian housing scheme was only established in 1939. (*The Durban Housing Survey*, op. cit., pp. 296–8. Chapter X gives an account of Indian housing.)

[3] *Ibid.*, p. 173. These estimates are approximate. The race of owner was established by the name, which is sometimes misleading.

C

Indian areas, incorporated into the City in 1932. It was
only at a late stage of the history of Durban that Indians
began to acquire properties in the more desirable European
areas of the Old Borough. This immediately led to European
agitation, the appointment of the 'penetration' commissions
and interim 'pegging' legislation.[1]

During the Second World War and immediately after,
the City Council proceeded with plans for racial zoning,
and made vigorous representations to the Government for
a four-point control, that is control of both residential and
trade premises in respect of both ownership and occupation.
In November 1950, some five months after the passing of
the Group Areas Act, the Council appointed a Technical
Sub-Committee which completed its task most expeditiously.
Of all the major cities in the Union, Durban, through its
City Council, has shown the greatest enthusiasm for compulsory segregation, and has indeed contributed to the
planning of Group Areas legislation for the country as
a whole.

The plans of the Technical Sub-Committee rest on the
basic proposition that contact between the races in residential areas breeds conflict. This proposition was implicit
in the mandate to plan residential Group Areas, but the
Technical Sub-Committee did not accept it without some
examination. However, the 'proof' offered in the following
paragraphs[2] is clearly anecdotal illustration, though presumably based on observations and conclusions not recorded
in this report. In any event, it carries the problem no
farther.

7. Residential segregation arises primarily from the
   desire of persons of the same group to live in the same

---

[1] See Chapter VI.
[2] *First Report of the Technical Sub-Committee on Race Zoning*, dated 22nd June
1951, pp. 5–6.

neighbourhood. Sometimes it occurs voluntarily, but where development has not been strictly controlled or has been piecemeal and *ad hoc*, a mixture of races occurs. Mixture may take the form:

Of sharing individual dwellings, e.g. poor Europeans hire rooms in Indian houses;
Of two or more races occupying separate but contiguous dwellings, e.g. Indians occupy a large number of houses in certain European areas such as Block AL; or
Of an island of one race in the area of one or more other races, e.g. Chesterville is a Native island surrounded by European and Indian properties.

8. The juxtaposition of races of different cultures has tended to produce conflict—not necessarily overt or manifesting itself at its geographic source, but often ultimately producing diffused inter-racial antipathy.[1]

9. Race differences may cause one group quite unwittingly to offend another. Europeans tend to dislike the very sight of a large number of people inhabiting a single house, however inoffensive the people are, and consequently react unfavourably to Indian neighbours whose communal family system involves the presence of many people in one house. Both Europeans and Indians are annoyed by the noise which appears to be inseparable from even small groups of Natives enjoying themselves or having ordinary conversations. When perfectly innocent traits of one race prove so annoying to other races, it

[1] This paragraph is of some interest since it removes the problem of the effects of race contact from the field of scientific study. If the conflict which arises from contact is not necessarily overt, and does not necessarily manifest itself at the point of contact, but may be covert and diffused, there is almost certain to be some inter-racial antipathy somewhere which may be produced as evidence to discount apparent harmony between neighbours of different races in a particular locality. This is especially so in South Africa where there is widespread inter-racial antipathy.

is not surprising that less innocent aspects such as traffic in illicit liquor, sexual relations between the races, or commercial competition between an emergent group such as Natives and a vested trading group such as Indians should produce deep-seated antagonisms.

10. However harmoniously an individual may get on with his neighbours of another race, and however free he and his particular property may be from those features which other races dislike, the sheer fact of his being of that race may, in a society where race feeling often runs high, be sufficient to make his presence distasteful to his neighbours.

11. It follows from these circumstances that residential neighbourhoods should not only be clearly defined, but should be such as to reduce the possibility of one group's spilling over into another's area, or of casually crossing the border.[1]

Having laid down that residential contact causes friction, the officials proceed to distinguish other types of contact. Friction, according to their view, arises not only from living together as neighbours or from loose residential contiguity, but even from the passage of members of one race through the living area of another. The degree of undesirability is said to vary with mode of travel. Most objectionable is the large-scale pedestrian movement of one race through the area of another, though vehicular traffic may be equally resented. Railway travel, being more or less sealed off, and

---

[1] The approach of the Technical Sub-Committee to the basic proposition that residential contact promotes conflict, contrasts sharply with the expert efficiency shown in the report as a whole. Sometimes, advocates of racial segregation cite the Durban riots of Africans against Indians in 1949 as an example of the dangers of residential contact. Others assert that the cause of the riots was not to be found in residential contact, that the rioters came largely from compounds and invaded the residential areas; and they cite examples of African residents who, at great personal risk, protected their Indian neighbours from assault.

roads, which serve as common highways segregated from the neighbouring areas, are relatively unobjectionable.

Inter-racial contact in industrial and commercial zones is differentiated from inter-racial contact in residential areas. The members of the Technical Sub-Committee consider the passage of one race through an industrial or central commercial area, operated by another race, as not open to the same objections, since business areas may be regarded as 'common', whether or not racially zoned. Indeed, they did not favour the immediate zoning of racially segregated business districts, being supported in this view by the Natal Employers' Association, the Natal Chamber of Industries and the Durban Chamber of Commerce on grounds of inconvenience, expense, unsuitable siting of factories, transport complications, and retardation of development. The Technical Sub-Committee suggested instead that an area might be given an orientation towards development by a particular racial group, but that the greatest flexibility should be retained. The formulation of rigid rules would be unwise at this stage.

Clearly, not only the type of contact but also the level of contact is involved in the distinction between residential and business areas. In residential areas, neighbours meet as equals in a relatively intimate sector of living. The equality is the crucial factor, not the racial intermingling, since the presence of domestic servants of a different race is not regarded as objectionable. In industrial areas, the relationship is usually on an unequal basis (namely between white employers and managers on the one hand, and non-white artisans and labourers on the other), and in both commercial and industrial areas the contact is fairly impersonal.

In any event, economic factors have a way of over-riding other considerations. The Technical Sub-Committee's description of the central commercial and industrial areas as 'common' is reminiscent of the principle applied in Indian caste society to allow for the employment of workers of different castes in the same organization. Both the artisan in his occupation, and the workshop itself, are ritually clean;[1] hence contact between workers of higher and lower castes in industrial employment is not polluting. The principle is clearly a rationalization of an economic compulsion over-riding the sentiments of caste pollution. So, too, the conclusions of the Sub-Committee reflect economic need. Indeed, the officials stress the economic interdependence of the races. European industry employs a predominance of Non-Europeans; some European shops, even in the most fashionable West Street, make special efforts to attract Non-European customers; conversely, Indian shops have no lack of European patrons, and some stalls at the Native Market rely very largely on a curio trade with Europeans. 'The economic interdependence of the races is thus such that in the central business area and in the industrial areas the streets will present a mixed racial picture, regardless of the race of the trader or industrialist.'[2]

The plans of the Technical Sub-Committee for racial segregation apply therefore to the residential areas. They are based on the propositions that residential segregation must be sufficiently effective to avoid contact between the races not only within each racial zone but also on the borders between them, and that the racial zones must be so designed as to discourage the movement of people of one race into the area of another. The plans are largely determined by the acceptance of these propositions.

Since 'effective segregation demands effective boundaries', the Sub-Committee favours such natural boundaries as the 'rivers, steep valleys, cliffs and hill tops', with which Durban abounds. Artificial barriers are considered less desirable, the most effective of these being a belt of industrial or commercial development, though railway lines are also useful. Narrow vacant green belts are regarded as unsatis-

[1] Gerth and Mills, *From Max Weber* (Oxford University Press, 1946), p. 412.
[2] *First Report of the Technical Sub-Committee on Race Zoning*, pp. 18–19.

factory, since they tend to become communal parks and thus encourage contact, but used open spaces reserved for one race, and large open spaces, are effective. A road may serve to separate groups, if it is zoned for non-residential purposes. Under no circumstances should people of different races face each other across a road: it is preferable to make the dividing line at the back-yards.

The general principle that one race should not be routed through the residential area of another profoundly affects the town plan. Each race needs access to place of work without traversing the residential areas of other races. Racial islands or pockets must therefore be avoided.[1] However, since the commercial and industrial districts may be deemed 'common', it is not necessary that residents should be able to move directly from their racial zones to their places of work. All they require is access to any point in the business area. Hence, the Technical Sub-Committee recommends a narrow ribbon-like elongation of industrial areas, a solution compatible with the topography of the city. Racial zones would then radiate from the commercial and industrial belt, and workers could move directly from their own zones into racially neutral areas.

If this radial plan is to succeed, then the racial zones, according to the view of the Technical Sub-Committee, must allow for expansion of the group into the hinterland, otherwise the careful arrangement of racial areas might be shattered by pressure of population. Racial zones should be large, partly because it is easier for the Police and Defence to protect and control them, but also because a measure of local self-government by Non-Europeans may be exercised more effectively. However, there is a limit placed on the size of the racial zone, namely that the extension into the hinterland cannot be carried to a point where the journey

[1] Alternatively, an underground railway or a helicopter service would provide a ready solution, since residents living in a racial island could then get to work without crossing other residential areas. A suggestion that a tunnel be constructed was not very seriously considered.

to work becomes excessive. This point will vary for the different racial groups, the more wealthy Europeans being in a better position to live at a long distance from place of work, or remote from public transport. Where the optimum point is likely to be exceeded, and the difficulties cannot be met by low-cost, efficient transport, the Sub-Committee recommends the establishment of additional zones, rather than the extension of a single zone.

These then are the principles which form the basis of the Durban town plan. They are summarized by the Sub-Committee as follows:

1. A residential race zone should:

   (a) have boundaries which should as far as possible constitute barriers of a kind preventing or discouraging contact between races in neighbouring residential zones;

   (b) have direct access to working areas and to such amenities as are used by all races, so that its residents do not have to traverse the residential areas of another race, or do so only by rail or by way of a common highway segregated from the residential areas abutting it;

   (c) be large enough to develop into an area of full or partial self-government or be substantially contiguous to such an area;

   (d) provide appropriate land for all economic and social classes which are present in the race group concerned, or may be expected to emerge in the course of time; and for group institutions, suburban shopping, minor industry and recreation;

   (e) be so sited that the means of transport most suitable for the group concerned is or can be made available.

2. The number of race zones not contiguous to zones occupied by the same race must be kept as low as

possible; accordingly large areas offering scope for urban expansion not too remote from the group's places of employment are to be preferred to areas that cannot be expanded.

3. In order to give the maximum length of common boundary between working areas and residential zones, and thus reduce transport costs and difficulties, dispersal of industry in ribbon formation where practicable is preferable to the massing of industry in great blocks.

4. In planning areas for each race group, the present and future requirements of the group, in relation to other groups, must be determining factors; the extent of situation of land presently owned, occupied or otherwise allocated to that group is not a material consideration.

5. Settled racially homogeneous communities should not be disturbed except in so far as it is necessary to give effect to the postulates set out above, but it is occupation and not mere ownership that constitutes settlement.

6. Different race groups may have differing needs in respect of building and site development. In allocating zones to each race, due account must be taken of the topographical suitability of the land and of the extent to which the race group concerned can effectively utilize existing sites and building development.

7. The central business area and the existing or potential industrial areas should not, in the initial stages, be earmarked for the exclusive use of any race, but should be so controlled as to permit orientation of different portions towards the appropriate groups.[1]

Analysis of these principles against the background of general Town Planning theory emphasizes the relatively

[1] *First Report of the Technical Sub-Committee on Race Zoning*, pp. 23–5.

unique character of the experiment in Durban. Town
Planners generally work on the assumption that contact
between residents promotes co-operation and community
development. The size of a residential neighbourhood is
often determined by two main considerations—that the
neighbourhood should be large enough for a socially balanced
population able to support an adequate provision of facilities,
but not so large that residents do not have the opportunity
for contact. Barriers may be used to increase contact within
a geographically defined area, perceived as such by the
residents. The assumption is that residents can more readily
perceive their suburbs as a whole, if the areas are clearly
defined, and that community sentiment is promoted by the
definition of the area of living; hence, the barriers may be
largely symbolic. The emphasis throughout is placed on
community development.

In Durban the Technical Sub-Committee did not ignore
community development. It was clearly thinking along the
lines of the urban neighbourhood centre when it referred to
the development of adequate shopping facilities as essential
for providing opportunity, self-sufficiency and a high degree
of community life. The desire to give a measure of local
autonomy in the Non-European racial zones was also an
important consideration. But the emphasis is on racial
separation—inevitably, since this was the Sub-Committee's
task—and the town plan is determined by the basic principle
of compulsory racial separation. The function of barriers
is not to stimulate community sentiment in a defined area,
but effectively to prevent contact between the races. It
is for this reason that the barriers must be real and formid-
able—rivers, steep valleys, cliffs and hilltops.

CHAPTER II

THE PEOPLES OF DURBAN:
ECONOMIC ASPECTS

The opening section of this chapter, dealing very briefly with
the sectors of the economy, is based on an analysis specially
prepared for us by Leo Katzen, Lecturer in Economics at the
University of Natal. T. J. D. Fair, in *The Distribution of Population in Natal* (Oxford University Press, 1955), discusses the
industrial population in Chapter V and the urban population
in Chapter VI. These chapters give the regional background
to the present analysis.

DURBAN attracts to its beaches, and to the many hotels
along the sea front and in the city, some 200,000
tourists a year. The presence of so many visitors
seeking recreation, the broad main streets lined with solid
buildings, the boulevards with their coloured lights, and
above all the leisured pace of life, give Durban the atmo-
sphere of a prosperous seaside resort.

The port itself has great beauty. Two ribs of land, the
steeply shelving Bluff and the Point, enclose a wide expanse
of sea. Ocean liners are always anchored there, and colourful
small craft, whalers, tankers, and yachts. A centre for fishing
and boating, and a link with the outside world, the port has
also played a major part in the growth of the city and
continues to be an important factor in its economy. Durban
handles today, as it did forty years ago, more cargo than all
the other Union ports taken together.[1]

The growth of the port was conditioned by the fact that

[1] Port Natal handled 3,051,346 tons of cargo in 1910 (59·68 per cent of the
total Union tonnage) and an average of 5,904,195 tons during the period
1946–52 (51·96 per cent of the Union total). See Reports of the General
Manager of the South African Railways and Harbours, 1946–52.

Durban has a large natural harbour which lies roughly midway between East London and Lourenço Marques. It is also the Union port nearest to South Africa's main industrial centre in the Witwatersrand and hence the most economic port for the handling of goods to and from this area, while proximity to the coal fields of Natal has favoured its development as the main coal-bunkering port in the Union.

Apart from the services normally associated with a port, such as stevedoring, storage and warehousing, forwarding agencies, brokerage, travel and tourist agencies, and railways, there are a number of industries whose growth has been stimulated directly by the existence of a large port. Durban is the home of the Union's most important ship-repairing industry, handling about 60 per cent of the ships that call for repairs at Union ports and employing between 1,500 and 1,800 men. With the selection of Durban as a port for ship repairs by three of the world's largest tank fleet companies, the industry is likely to expand rapidly. This selection, again, is linked with the establishment of the new oil refinery, a second major industry closely connected with the port, and other industries will probably develop to use the by-products resulting from the refining of crude oils. Finally, a large fertilizer industry, based on imported raw materials, has grown up in Durban, and six of the Union's thirteen fertilizer factories are located there.

Durban today is the third largest city in South Africa,[1] and a centre for many economic activities either unconnected or only indirectly connected with the port. A broad picture of these activities is given in Table I showing the industrial distribution of the population. Services occupy the largest group of the city's working population, then industry,

[1] The 1951 Union Population Census, U.G. 42/1955, gives the population of Johannesburg as 631,911, of Cape Town as 441,209, and of Durban as 432,670. The figure for Durban exceeds the total population shown in the special Census tabulations prepared for us by the Director of Census. Our own figures exclude harbour and shipping personnel, and a small, relatively undeveloped, portion of Durban. *Unless otherwise stated, our calculations are based on the data we received from the Director of Census.*

TABLE 1

INDUSTRIAL DISTRIBUTION OF THE POPULATION, DURBAN: 1951 CENSUS

	Europeans		Coloureds		Indians		Africans		Total	Percentage of Economically Active Population
	Males	Females	Males	Females	Males	Females	Males	Females		
Agriculture, forestry, hunting and fishing	420	20	84	—	1,279	70	861	45	2,779	1·94
Mining and quarrying	418	78	7	—	43	—	564	—	1,110	
Manufacturing	11,049	3,071	1,565	1,256	10,643	585	19,374	183	47,726	32·27 (Industry)
Construction	4,314	118	461	2	934	2	10,116	40	15,987	
Electricity, gas, water and sanitary services	464	41	5	—	89	—	421	1	1,021	
Commerce	7,654	6,046	215	38	6,070	299	10,557	198	31,077	15·49 (Commerce)
Transport, storage and communication	7,660	922	293	3	1,453	14	10,597	14	20,956	10·45 (Transport)
Services	7,922	5,863	400	701	7,691	967	28,196	16,790	68,530	34·17 (Services)
Activities not adequately described	1,398	576	791	193	6,486	535	1,397	20	11,396	5·68
Non-economic activities	22,560	50,699	3,900	6,575	39,815	69,208	11,381	25,524	229,662	
TOTAL	63,859	67,434	7,721	8,768	74,503	71,680	93,464	42,815	430,244	

(handwritten annotations near Total column: 64,734   3,889)

NOTE.—Numbers engaged are normally a fairly good indicator of the economic significance of a particular sector, but must be used with a certain amount of caution, especially where the sector includes a wide variety of occupations and skills. This is particularly important in South Africa where the discrepancy in skill, earnings and economic opportunity as between European and Non-European is so considerable. Net income or output is a better indicator of economic significance, but statistics of income and output are more meagre than those of numbers engaged.

commerce, and transport. The large number engaged in services is, however, misleading, since about 40 per cent of service workers are African domestic servants in private households earning relatively low wages. Unfortunately, general statistics of income are too incomplete for reliable estimates of the economic significance of the services in Durban.

In the sector of Commerce the total value of trade has increased considerably in recent years. The 1946–7 Census showed 2,424 wholesale and retail establishments in Durban, employing 26,768 people with a net income before tax of £14,677,000 (salaries and wages, £6,453,000; and net profit before tax, £8,224,000). Total sales were £61,346,000 for the wholesale trade and £35,843,000 for the retail trade. In 1952 the total value of retail sales was £57,705,000,[1] an increase of about 60 per cent in value terms between 1946–47 and 1952,[2] while the numbers engaged in the commercial sector as a whole had increased about 16 per cent by 1951.

Industry is certainly the most important sector of the economy of Durban, which ranks as the third main industrial centre in the Union. Yet notwithstanding the many advantages Durban enjoys in its port—abundant and cheap African labour in the reserves of Natal, a relatively plentiful water-supply and proximity to the Witwatersrand—there is little evidence of any large-scale specialization in basic industries dependent on imported raw materials. In all the groups of industries shown in Table II, the number of factories in Durban is less than the number in either the Southern Transvaal or the Western Cape or in both these areas, and, in most cases, the industry in the Durban area is a duplication, on a smaller scale, of that in the two major industrial centres.

---

[1] This is the only figure available from the 1952 Census of Wholesale and Retail Establishments. A recent figure of £64,000,000 for total retail sales in 1955 has been given by the Census Office (*Sunday Tribune*, 15th January 1956, p. 11).

[2] Or an increase of about 18 per cent in real terms when deflating the 1952 figure by the increase in retail prices.

NUMBER OF FACTORIES IN THE UNION AND IN CERTAIN INDUSTRIAL AREAS FOR EACH INDUSTRIAL CLASS (PRIVATE INDUSTRIES ONLY): 1949/50

Industry	Union	Cape Western	Port Elizabeth and Uttenhage	Durban and Pinetown	Southern Transvaal
1 Treatment of raw materials, the products of agriculture, etc.	74	10	9	8	19
2 Processes in stone, clay, earthenware and glass	681	79	45	32	180
3 Working in wood	667	76	34	46	178
4 Metal, engineering works, etc.	2,228	327	92	202	1,003
5 Preparation of food, drink and tobacco	2,454	239	58	94	297
6 Production of clothing and textiles (excluding shoes)	1,487	298	75	207	607
7 Books, paper, printing and bookbinding	548	120	28	60	182
8 Vehicle erection and repairs	2,793	246	73	138	560
9 Ship- and boat-building and repairing	18	7	—	5	2
10 Furniture, bedding and upholstery	499	83	19	59	207
11 Drugs, chemicals, paints, varnishes, fertilizers, etc.	329	58	19	63	143
12 Scientific apparatus	43	12	2	4	19
13 Jewellery, timepieces, plated ware	166	27	3	36	85
14 Heat, light and power	128	4	2	7	13
15 Leather and leatherware	447	85	37	56	124
16 Building and contracting	1,560	230	66	121	428
17 Other industries	186	28	13	23	63
Total	14,308	1,928	575	1,161	4,110

SOURCE.—*Census of Industrial Establishments*, 1947–8, 48–9, 49–50 (U.G. No. 30/1954, pp. 36 et seq.).

NOTE.—The number of factories is a crude index, and the large groupings in Table II conceal differences in particular industries, as, for example, in the ship-repairing, fertilizer and oil-refining industries. Durban also has an important share in the textile, paint and timber industries, though even in these industries there are more factories in either the Southern Transvaal or the Western Cape. If we use as a base Durban's share in the total Union output, and measure its contribution to each industry against this base, then it is clear that, within Durban, there is a relative concentration in the chemical, textile and rubber industries.

Railway rating policies are an important reason for this comparative lack of specialization. The rates discriminate in favour of bulky, low value, unprocessed or semi-processed raw materials and against high-value manufactured goods. This has meant, other things being equal, that it usually pays to ship the raw product from the point of production or of entry to manufacturing centres near the main markets. The discriminatory tariff thus makes it possible to concentrate on the Witwatersrand industries which could not otherwise be operated economically at a considerable distance from the port. Moreover, the advantage Durban has over other Union ports because of proximity to the Witwatersrand is largely discounted by a higher railway tariff. These policies also partly explain the relatively slow industrial development of Durban in the past.

The Second World War, however, stimulated industrial development, and the numbers both of establishments and of industrial workers in the Durban–Pinetown metropolitan region increased rapidly. Using the figures of the Industrial Census as our basis, we estimate the net output in 1950–1 of those engaged in the industries of Durban, and living either in Durban or in the metropolitan area, as between £38 and £40 million, and the gross output as a little over £100 million. Since 1951, expansion has continued, and, in February 1956, there were 1,458 factories in Durban and 95 in Pinetown,[1] as compared with a combined total of 1,161 in 1949–50.

[1] Information supplied by the Department of Labour. The figure of 1,458 factories includes factories in construction, and the permanent workshops of Builders and Contractors, while the Industrial Census figure of 1,161 excludes factories in construction, but includes all Builders and Contractors.

SOURCES FOR TABLE III, OPPOSITE.—1938–9 figures derived from *Census of Industrial Establishments* 1941–2, *U.G.* 20/1945.

1945–6, 1946–7, 1949–50 *Census of Industrial Establishments* 1947–8, 1948–9, 1949–50, *U.G.* 30/1950.

1950–1, 1951–2 *Special Report* 206. *Thirty-fifth Industrial Census* 1951–2 (*Preliminary Report*).

TABLE III

INDUSTRIAL ESTABLISHMENTS, EMPLOYEES
AND NET OUTPUT FOR THE DURBAN–PINETOWN
METROPOLITAN AREA, 1938–1952: INDUSTRIAL
CENSUS

| YEAR | NUMBER OF ESTABLISHMENTS | EMPLOYEES (all races) | | NET OUTPUT £1,000s |
		NUMBERS OF EMPLOYEES	INDEX	
1938–9	863	38,499	100	11,204
1945–6	934	58,894	153	24,461
1946–7	947	60,049	156	27,396
1949–50	1,191	78,888	205	40,722
1950–1	1,154*	71,768*		42,814*
1951–2	1,120*	75,096*		48,167*

*Private Industries only

NOTE 1.—The Industrial Census includes the whole of the Durban
and Pinetown area and is therefore not comparable with the industrial
distribution of the Durban population shown in Table I. Moreover,
Table I is derived from the Population Census, and allowance must
therefore be made for under-enumeration, due to the failure of persons,
particularly Africans 'illegally' in Durban, to fill in the Census forms.
Then, too, a certain proportion of the 11,396 persons whose activities
were not adequately described in the Population Census must certainly
be industrial workers.

2. For the year 1950–1 there were 71,768 people engaged in private
industry in the Durban–Pinetown area. To this figure must be added
approximately another 13,000 engaged in central and local government
enterprises. In the metropolitan area as a whole there were therefore
about 20,000 industrial workers in excess of the figures given in the
Population Census for Durban alone. Our estimate of net and gross
industrial output in Durban is based on the assumption that about
10,000 of Durban's industrial workers live in the metropolitan area
outside the borough. This seems a reasonable estimate, since the only
other industrial areas in the metropolitan region are those of Pinetown
and New Germany, which are still relatively small.

3. The net output figure given in the Industrial Census is gross output
less cost of materials used and cost of fuel, light and power. It would,
therefore, be somewhat larger than the true net output (or income)
figure for this sector, which would still have to take into account allow-
ances for depreciation of capital, rent, interest charges, selling costs, etc.

D

Durban has now begun to exploit its natural advantages. Many economists expect that the most rapid industrial expansion will take place in the province of Natal as a whole. There is still industrial land available in Durban itself, while the development of the metropolitan region is in its early phase. The City of Durban therefore has great opportunities to enhance its significance in the economy of the Union. The extent to which it realizes these opportunities will depend largely on the use made of the available labour resources of all races.

The racial composition of Durban is unique among the major cities of the Union in two respects. First, there is a concentration of Indians within its boundaries: 40·16 per cent of the total South African Indian population[1] lives in Durban, as compared with 5·01 per cent Europeans, 1·51 per cent Coloureds and 1·57 per cent Africans. And second, Europeans, Indians and Africans are represented in almost equal proportions (between 30 per cent and 34 per cent), with Indians as the largest group.

The proportion of Europeans in Durban is appreciably lower than in other South African cities with a population of over 150,000. Johannesburg has 54·17 per cent Europeans, Cape Town 42·33 per cent, Pretoria 56·81 per cent and Port Elizabeth 41·68 per cent.[2] This lower proportion of Europeans in the population may be attributed partly to the fact that the Indians of Durban carry out some of the functions of Europeans in contemporary South African urban society.

The first settlement in Durban, in 1824, was made by British settlers, attracted by opportunities for trade with the

[1] The Census figures are for Asiatics, but the number of Asiatics, other than Indians, in the Union as a whole is very small. The main migration of Indians was to Natal, and the restrictions on inter-provincial movement bottled them in that province.

[2] Calculations based on Special Report No. 200, 1951 Census.

interior. During the 1830s the population amounted to about thirty or more white persons, largely traders and hunters, and several hundred Africans, most of them probably refugees from the Zulu wars.[1] In 1854, when Durban was granted its municipal charter, the European population had grown to 1,204.[2] No figures are available for Africans, and Indian immigrants only began to arrive

TABLE IV

RACE COMPOSITION OF THE DURBAN
POPULATION: 1951 CENSUS

RACE	NUMBER	PERCENTAGE
Europeans . . .	131,293	30·51
Coloureds . . .	16,489	3·83
Indians . . .	146,183	33·98
Africans . . .	136,279	31·68
TOTAL . .	430,244	100·00

in 1860. From 1862 until 1902 Durban Municipality carried out a yearly census: thereafter, the City Health Department provided yearly estimates of the population, save in those years when a Government Census was taken. Annual population figures, by estimate and census, are therefore available from 1862, and in Figure 2 we have used them to show the rate of growth of the total population of Durban and of its constituent racial groups.

Population growth, stimulated by the discovery of gold

[1] A. F. Hattersley, *The British Settlement of Natal* (Cambridge University Press, 1950), pp. 13–14. For a description of the fortunes of the early town, see also Hattersley, *Portrait of a Colony: The Story of Natal* (Cambridge University Press, 1940) and *The Natalians* (Pietermaritzburg, Shuter and Shooter, 1940).
[2] According to an estimate given by W. P. M. Henderson, *Durban: Fifty Years Municipal History* (Durban, Robinson & Co., 1904), p. 3.

on the Witwatersrand in 1884 and the two world wars, has been very rapid. The European trend corresponds closely to that of the total population, suggesting that European development shaped the pattern of Durban's growth. The increase in African population follows the European trend, though the stimulus of the two world wars is more marked, indicating the greater use of African man-power, relative to European, as a result of industrial expansion. Coloureds are shown for the first time in 1902 as 747 persons; prior to that date they were included in the European population. The count of Coloureds fluctuates wildly until about 1910, and then follows a normal growth pattern, apart from a decline in the middle 1920s, probably due to inadequate enumeration.

The rates of increase for the Indian population were appreciably higher than those of the Africans or Europeans in the early period of indentures, until about 1880, when they begin to follow more or less the same trend. Then, from the time of the first world war and in marked contrast to the European and especially the African population, the number of Indians declines, returning to pre-war strength only in 1931–2. The repatriation of Indians certainly contributed to the slowing down of their population growth, but the major factor must have been their movement to areas on the fringes of the Borough. When, in 1932, the boundaries of the city were extended, the Indian population more than trebled as a result of the addition of about 50,000 Indians, while the European and African groups each increased only by some 20,000. The rate of Indian population growth in the city was masked by settlement in the peri-urban areas. In the last few years the rate of Indian increase was somewhat higher than that of the European.

In contrast to the numerical equality of the main racial groups in Durban and the rough approximation in rates of growth, their participation in the economic life of Durban and their demographic characteristics are very different.

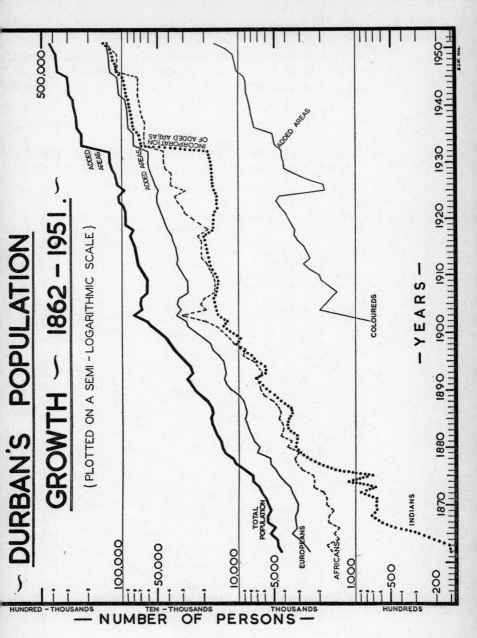

FIGURE 2

The Africans constitute the working base of the population, contributing 99,375 persons to the total labour force of 200,593; that is to say, they are 49·54 per cent of the labour

TABLE V

OCCUPATIONAL DISTRIBUTION OF THE POPULATION OF DURBAN: 1951 CENSUS

OCCUPATIONAL CATEGORY	ABSOLUTE NUMBERS			
	Europeans	*Coloureds*	*Indians*	*Africans*
1. Professional, Technical and Related Workers .	6,375	232	1,130	1,263
2. Managers, Administrators and Officials* .	5,099	32	2,182	233
3. Clerical, Office and Related Workers .	16,741	95	1,647	913
4. Salesmen and Related Workers . . .	4,812	73	3,235	690
5. Farmers, Fishermen, Hunters and Related Workers . . .	350	58	1,516	1,202
6. Mine, Quarry and Related Workers . .	194	5	26	529
7. Workers in Operating Transport Occupations	1,979	348	1,650	2,876
8. Craftsmen, Factory-Operatives, Manual Workers, Labourers .	17,479	3,661	15,345	53,906
9. Services and Related Workers . . .	3,302	803	4,914	36,326
10. Other and Unidentifiable . . .	1,704	711	5,520	1,437
11. Not Gainfully Employed	73,258	10,471	109,018	36,904
TOTAL . .	131,293	16,489	146,183	136,279

* Excluding Farming and Mining.

NOTE.—The unemployed were coded under their usual occupations, so that categories 1–10 include also unemployed persons.

force, though only 31·68 per cent of the whole population. In one occupational category alone, that of *Craftsmen, Factory Operatives, Manual Workers, Labourers* (Table V), the number of Africans is almost equal to the entire European labour force and exceeds that of the Indian and Coloured combined (categories 1–10). The percentage of working to total population for each race is as follows: African, 72·92 per cent; European, 44·21 per cent; Coloured, 36·50 per cent; and Indian, 25·42 per cent.

The different levels of work for the racial groups are shown in Table VI, which gives the distribution of each racial group in the ten broad occupational categories of the Census. The first four categories—professional, managerial, clerical and sales—are the traditional occupations of Europeans in South Africa. Over half the working European population of Durban—56·91 per cent—is engaged in these occupations. The corresponding figure for Africans is 3·11 per cent. Categories 8 and 9—craftsmen, factory operatives, manual workers, labourers, domestic and other servants—include the traditional unskilled and semi-skilled manual occupations of the Africans. The percentage of European workers in these occupations in Durban is 35·81 as compared with a percentage for Africans of 90·81. Of the four groups, the Europeans have the largest proportion of their workers in 'white collar' employment, and the smallest in manual work, in direct contrast to the occupational distribution of Africans. The two groups clearly complement each other's activities.

The Indian population is in an intermediate position between European and African, having 22·05 per cent in the 'white collar' occupations, and 54·51 per cent in the manual and service occupations. The proportion of Indian workers classified as salesmen and related workers—8·70 per cent as compared with 8·29 per cent of European workers[1]—indicates the extent to which Indians have

---

[1] In absolute numbers there are more Europeans in this category than Indians—4,812 as compared with 3,235.

entered into the field of commerce. Indians participate at both the European and African levels of the economy. The Coloureds are relatively less concentrated in the manual work and service categories than the Africans—74·18 per

TABLE VI

PERCENTAGE DISTRIBUTION OF OCCUPATIONS WITHIN EACH RACE, DURBAN: 1951 CENSUS

OCCUPATIONAL CATEGORY	PERCENTAGES			
	Europeans	Coloureds	Indians	Africans
1. Professional, Technical and Related Workers .	10·98	3·86	3·04	1·27
2. Managers, Administrators and Officials .	8·79	0·53	5·87	0·23
3. Clerical, Office and Related Workers .	28·85	1·58	4·44	0·92
4. Salesmen and Related Workers . . .	8·29	1·21	8·70	0·69
5. Farmers, Fishermen, Hunters, Lumbermen, etc. . . .	0·60	0·96	4·08	1·21
6. Mine, Quarry and Related Workers . .	0·33	0·08	0·07	0·53
7. Workers in Operating Transport Occupations	3·41	5·79	4·44	2·89
8. Craftsmen, Factory Operatives, Manual Workers, Labourers, etc. . . .	30·12	60·84	41·29	54·26
9. Services and Related Workers . . .	5·69	13·34	13·22	36·55
10. Other* and Unidentifiable . . .	2·94	11·81	14·85	1·45
TOTAL . .	100·00	100·00	100·00	100·00

* This category includes members of the armed forces, consular personnel, unemployed, African chiefs and headmen.

cent of their workers as compared with an African concentration of 90·81 per cent—and are employed more in the professional, managerial, clerical and sales categories—7·18 per cent as compared with 3·11 per cent. The broad hierarchy of employment among Non-Europeans, in terms of approximation to European patterns, is in the order Indians, Coloureds, Africans.

When we analyse each occupational category separately, and calculate the racial distribution of employees in that category (Table VII), the largely European character of the 'white collar' occupations is shown more clearly. Europeans are 70·83 per cent of the professional, technical and related workers; 67·57 per cent of the managerial group; 86·31 per cent of office workers; and 54·62 per cent of salesmen. Of the Non-European groups, only the Indians constitute an appreciable proportion of workers in any of these categories—28·92 per cent of the managerial class, and 36·72 per cent of the salesmen. In each of the Census categories 5–9—mainly occupations involving manual work —Africans provide a large proportion of workers, ranging from 38·45 per cent in farming and fishing to 80·11 per cent of service workers. The high proportion of 48·50 per cent Indians in category 5—farmers, fishermen, hunters—shows the extent to which the Indians of Durban are occupied in market gardening,[1] and in small fishing enterprises, often owned by a family or a group of families.

The broad classification of occupations in the Tables understates the wide differences between the races in level of employment. The professional category includes judges, acrobats and sports officials in its list of 78 occupations: clerical, office and related workers refer not only to accountants and stenographers, but also to telegraph messengers and office boys, while a salesman may be a newspaper boy or an estate agent. Selected occupations within the broad

---

[1] C. A. Woods, in *The Indian Community of Natal* (Oxford University Press, 1954, p. 23), quotes an estimate of 500 Indian market gardeners in 1949.

TABLE VII

PERCENTAGE DISTRIBUTION OF OCCUPATIONAL CATEGORIES BETWEEN THE FOUR RACES, DURBAN: 1951 CENSUS

OCCUPATIONAL CATEGORY	PERCENTAGE OF TOTAL IN CATEGORY				
	Europeans	*Coloureds*	*Indians*	*Africans*	*Total*
1. Professional, Technical and Related Workers	70·83	2·58	12·56	14·03	100·00
2. Managers, Administrators and Officials	67·57	0·42	28·92	3·09	100·00
3. Clerical, Office and Related Workers	86·31	0·49	8·49	4·71	100·00
4. Salesmen and Related Workers	54·62	0·83	36·72	7·83	100·00
5. Farmers, Fishermen, Hunters and Related Workers	11·20	1·85	48·50	38·45	100·00
6. Mine, Quarry and Related Workers	25·73	0·66	3·45	70·16	100·00
7. Operating Transport Workers	28·88	5·08	24·08	41·96	100·00
8. Craftsmen, Factory Operatives, Labourers, Manual Workers, etc.	19·34	4·05	16·98	59·63	100·00
9. Services and Related Workers	7·28	1·77	10·84	80·11	100·00
10. Other and Unidentifiable	18·18	7·59	58·90	15·33	100·00
11. Not Gainfully Employed	31·90	4·56	47·47	16·07	100·00

categories are more discriminating. Thus, at the higher professional levels, there are relatively fewer Non-Europeans, as is shown in the following comparison between the racial distribution of lawyers, barristers, doctors and dentists on the one hand, and of all professional workers on the other hand.

	Europeans	Coloureds	Indians	Africans
Lawyers, Barristers, Doctors, Dentists .	91·75%(578)	0·47%(3)	6·83%(43)	0·95%(6) [1]
All Professional Workers . .	70·83%	2·58%	12·56%	14·03%

Similarly, we can demonstrate the more favoured position of the European manual worker, particularly in relation to Indians and Africans, by comparing the distribution of metal workers (largely skilled) with the distribution of craftsmen, factory operatives, labourers and manual workers (category 8).

	Europeans	Coloureds	Indians	Africans
Metal Workers [2]	78·38%(4,955)	10·72%(678)	9·92%(627)	0·98%(62)
Craftsmen, Factory Operatives, Labourers and Manual Workers .	19·34%	4·05%	16·98%	59·63%

Conversely, the percentage of Africans increases, and that of other races decreases, when the distribution of domestic workers in private households is compared with the overall distribution of service employees.

	Europeans	Coloureds	Indians	Africans
Domestic Service	0·75%(223)	1·36%(402)	2·50%(738)	95·39%(28,208)
Services and Related Workers .	7·28%	1·77%	10·84%	80·11%

---

[1] Our figure of 6 African lawyers, barristers, doctors and dentists in 1951 is an estimate, while the figures for the other racial groups are derived from the Census. Our estimate of 6 is certainly too high: there are only 2 African doctors and 1 lawyer now practising in Durban, and no dentists or barristers.

[2] Occupations Nos. 700–740 of the Census Department's Code List.

The relatively poorly paid occupation of domestic servant is almost entirely African and, in contrast to other races, almost half the African domestic servants are men—46·19 per cent of African domestic servants as compared with 0·45 per cent of European, 6·97 per cent of Coloured, and 28·59 per cent of Indian.

Status of employment (employer, employee, unemployed) gives a further index of level of participation in the economy of Durban. Unfortunately, this information was not gathered for Africans in the Census, so that Table VIII deals only with Europeans, Coloureds and Indians.

An urban African employer class has only developed in recent years, and its numbers are certainly very small.[1] Only 1·33 per cent of the Coloured working population is of employer status, as compared with a European percentage of 6·47. Indians have the largest proportion of working population in the employer class (6·87 per cent), though the absolute number of Indian employers is less than that of Europeans (2,548 as compared with 3,752). This Indian sharing of employer status with Europeans is related to the relatively high proportion of Indians in the occupational category of salesmen (see Table VII, p. 58), and to the many small retail stores in the Indian section of the city. There are relatively few large Indian enterprises, and the equating of employers in Table VIII, irrespective of the numbers employed, overstates the role of Indians as employers of labour.[2]

Indians also have the highest proportion of persons working for their own account, but not employing anyone. The respective figures are 5·63 per cent for Indians, 1·53 per cent

[1] There were 325 Trading Licences held by Africans in Durban during 1951. On the assumption that an average of two licences were issued for each business, there would have been about 162 African traders.

[2] Information is not available as to the number of workers employed by employers of each race. Woods, op. cit., p. 19, states that a safe over-all average figure for assistants in Indian trading establishments throughout Natal would not be more than two per business. The average figure may be somewhat higher in the more highly developed commercial centre of Durban.

TABLE VIII

STATUS OF EMPLOYMENT OF POPULATION, DURBAN: 1951 CENSUS

Status of Employment	Absolute Numbers			Percentages		
	Europeans	Coloureds	Indians	Europeans	Coloureds	Indians
Employer	3,752	80	2,548	6·47	1·33	6·87
Own Account (i.e. not employing any-one)	841	92	2,092	1·45	1·53	5·63
Employee	51,448	4,871	25,252	88·67	81·01	67·96
Family Worker (i.e. assisting relative)	9	1	107	0·02	0·02	0·29
Unemployed (previously employed)	1,621	813	5,656	2·79	13·52	15·23
Unemployed (looking for first job)	7	12	57	0·01	0·20	0·15
Trainee (not apprentice)	34	—	—	0·06	—	—
Unspecified	309	144	1,437	0·53	2·39	3·87
TOTAL*	58,021	6,013	37,149	100·00	100·00	100·00

* There are small differences between the totals in this Table, and the totals for the occupational dis-tribution of the population (categories 1–10, in Table V, p. 54). These differences are not explained by the inclusion in this Table of persons seeking employment for the first time.

for Coloureds, and 1·45 per cent Europeans. Many of these Indian workers are hawkers, pedlars, gardeners, handymen and craftsmen. The large numbers in this occupational category may be an adjustment to the difficulty of securing employment. About 1 in every 7 of the Indian working population was unemployed at the time of the 1951 Census. The more favourable employment opportunities for Europeans are shown by the fact that they have the highest proportion of their workers in the category of employees (Europeans 88·67 per cent, Coloureds 81·01 per cent, Indians 67·96 per cent), the lowest unemployed (2·79 per cent as compared with 13·52 per cent Coloureds and 15·23 per cent Indians), and the lowest proportion self-employed.

Wide differences in income are associated with the different occupational patterns of the races. Income data were not collected for Africans in the 1951 Census, and only the income distribution of Europeans, Coloureds and Indians is shown in Tables IX and X. These are included in Appendix A, while relevant data derived from the Tables are presented here in Figure 3. The pie diagrams show the proportion of each racial group in receipt of income. The histograms give the distribution of annual income in each racial group.

It is clear from the pie diagrams that the Europeans have the highest proportion of persons in receipt of income (over one-half), next the Coloureds (almost a third), and least the Indians (less than one-quarter). Or, to phrase the comparison in terms of the number of dependants, the Indians have the highest dependency rate (357 dependants to every 100 persons receiving income), the Europeans the lowest (95 dependants), while the Coloureds occupy an intermediate position (213 dependants per 100). The low proportion of Indian women receiving income contributes greatly to the high dependency rates. For every 100 Indian women in receipt of income, there are 2,404 female

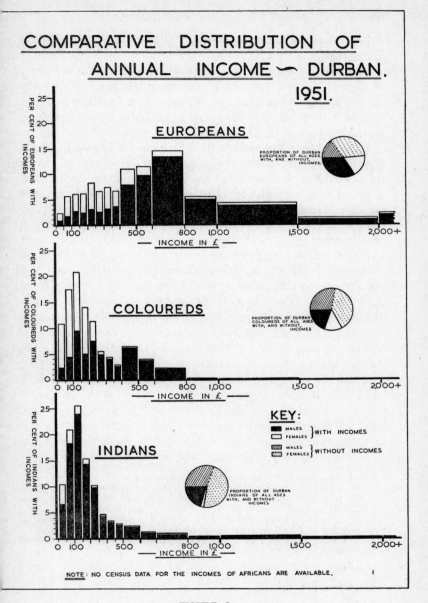

COMPARATIVE DISTRIBUTION OF ANNUAL INCOME — DURBAN, 1951.

FIGURE 3

dependants, as compared with 305 Coloureds and 192 Europeans.[1]

The histograms in Figure 3 show that the great majority of Coloureds and Indians in receipt of income receive less than £250 per annum; the relevant figures are 74·52 per cent of Coloureds and 82·73 per cent Indians, as compared with 28·46 per cent Europeans.

The modal income range for Europeans is between £400–£799: 37·11 per cent of European income earners are in this category, and only 12·54 per cent of Coloured and 4·74 per cent of Indian.[2] In the highest income range, the disparity between the races becomes more marked. Of the total number of Europeans in receipt of income, 13·85 per cent receive £800 and over, in contrast to 0·33 per cent Coloureds and 1·35 per cent Indians.[3]

In Table XI we have calculated the ratio between the percentage of Coloureds and Indians in each income category and the percentage of Europeans. Thus, reading the first row, the percentage of Indians in receipt of income, who earn less than £250, is almost 3 times as high as the European percentage, while the relevant ratio for the Coloureds is 2·62. As the income range is raised, the ratio declines sharply. Reading down the columns, the ratio for Coloureds falls from 2·62 in the range under £250, to 0·02 in the range over £800, while the Indian ratio falls from 2·91 to 0·10. The Indians, that is to say, are more concentrated in the extreme ranges than the Coloureds,[4] a further indication

[1] In calculating these dependency rates, we excluded the category of 'unspecified'—Table IX, Appendix A. The African population, as a largely working population, has the highest percentage employed (72·92 per cent). The dependency rate, excluding dependants outside Durban, is only 37·14 (the dependency rate in this case being calculated as the number of persons not gainfully employed, per 100 workers, including unemployed—Table V).

[2] The absolute figures are Europeans 24,843, Indians 1,509—a ratio of 16 Europeans to 1 Indian—and Coloureds 655 (Table IX, Appendix A).

[3] The absolute numbers are Europeans 9,274, Indians 431—a ratio of over 21:1—and Coloureds 17.

[4] Coefficients of relative variability $\left(\dfrac{\text{Standard deviation}}{\text{mean}} \times 100 \right)$ are Indians 136·3, and Coloureds 81·4.

that the Indians participate in the economy of Durban at two levels—the European level of managers, salesmen and employers, and the African level of manual work.

TABLE XI

COMPARISON OF INCOME DISTRIBUTION BETWEEN THE RACES: RATIO (Percentage of Coloureds or Indians in Receipt of Income/Percentage of Europeans) FOR SELECTED INCOME CATEGORIES, DURBAN: 1951 CENSUS

INCOME £ PER ANNUM	RATIOS	
	Coloured	Indian
Under 250 . . .	2·62	2·91
250–399 . . .	0·61	0·54
400–799 . . .	0·34	0·13
800+ . . .	0·02	0·10

Table XII summarizes for Europeans, Coloureds and Indians the income data of the 1951 Census in terms of the mean income of persons in receipt of income, and the *per capita* income. Since income data from Africans were not collected in the Census, we have made our own estimate.

European mean income (£552·06) is between 2 to 3 times as high as Indian and Coloured. The disparity between *per capita* incomes is more marked, since Coloureds and Indians have higher dependency rates.[1] The *per capita* income of Indians (£40·02) is particularly low, less than two-thirds that of the Coloureds, though the difference between the mean incomes is only some 10 per cent. The average income of Africans is lowest of all, £86 per annum according to our estimates. The *per capita* income is difficult

---

[1] The median age of the Coloureds is 18·86, of the Indians 16·18 (Table XIV).

E

to estimate, since many Africans support dependants living in reserves outside Durban. Our estimate (£45) is based on an assumption as to the amount of money sent into the reserves by Africans working in Durban, and is therefore not strictly comparable with the calculations based on the Census. Nevertheless, it seems likely that the *per capita* incomes available to the Africans and to the majority of the Indians are of roughly the same dimensions.

TABLE XII

MEAN AND *PER CAPITA* INCOME BY RACE, DURBAN, 1951

RACE	MEAN INCOME £ PER ANNUM	*Per Capita* INCOME £ PER ANNUM
Europeans . . .	552·06	282·74
Coloureds	201·20	64·34
Indians*	182·85	40·02
Africans (estimate) . .	87·00	45·00
	105.00	58.00

SOURCE.—Europeans, Coloureds and Indians—1951 Census. Africans —Estimate (Appendix A).

* Includes the small Chinese-speaking group of 73 persons. The mean income of £182·85 and *per capita* income of £40·02 are very close to the figures derived by Woods, op. cit., Table IV, opposite p. 52, from a sample house-to-house survey among Indians in Natal. His figures are monthly mean income—£15 5s. 4d. (£183 4s. per annum) and monthly *per capita* income—£3 4s. 3d. (£38 11s. per annum).

NOTE.—The final class in the Table of Income Distribution is £5,000+. In calculating the mean and *per capita* incomes, the midpoint of this class was estimated at £8,850, on the basis of income subject to supertax, earned by married and unmarried persons in the income class of over £5,000 per annum, for the tax year ending June 1951 (*Report of the Commissioner for Inland Revenue*, U.G. 67/1952). The estimate is based on returns for the Union as a whole, since separate figures were not available for Durban.

CHAPTER III

THE PEOPLES OF DURBAN (CONTD): AGE, SEX, MARITAL STATUS, BIRTH AND DEATH RATES, RELIGION, LANGUAGE; VARIATIONS BETWEEN AND WITHIN RACES

WIDE differences in age and sex composition, marital status, birth and death rates, are associated with the different roles of the races in the economy of Durban. Since Africans are engaged primarily in manual occupations, there has been selective migration of men from the reserves. At the same time, under the migratory labour system, official policies discourage urbanization and urban family life. In consequence, the African population has a disproportionate number of men, 218 males to every 100 females (see Table XIII). It is, however, becoming increasingly urbanized, and the sex ratio is moving towards parity. In 1892, the first year in which the municipal census for Durban gave separate figures for African men and women, there were 6,663 men and 396 women, a sex ratio of 16·82 as compared with the 1951 ratio of 2·18.[1]

Again, as a largely labouring population, Africans are

---

[1] The same trend, the result of increasing industrialization, is to be seen in all the major cities of the Union, as the figures below indicate.

African Sex Ratio			1921	1946
Cape Town	.	. .	3·94	2·26
Johannesburg	.	. .	8·45	2·43
Port Elizabeth	.	. .	1·27	1·04
Pretoria	.	. .	2·86	2·11
Durban	.	. .	6·28	2·66

(*Census Report*, U.G. 51/1949, pp. 78 et seq.)

concentrated in the years of able-bodied vigour. Their age structure does not correspond to any of the 'normal' age distributions of population,[1] largely as a result of the migratory labour system, but influenced also by the common

TABLE XIII

SEX COMPOSITION OF DURBAN'S POPULATION: 1951 CENSUS

SEX	RACE				TOTAL
	Europeans	Coloureds	Indians	Africans	
Male . .	63,859	7,721	74,503	93,464	239,547
Female . .	67,434	8,768	71,680	42,815	190,697
TOTAL .	131,293	16,489	146,183	136,279	430,244
Sex Ratio . .	0·95	0·88	1·04	2·18	1·26

practice of sending young children back to the reserves, where they can be brought up in the traditions of their people. Only about one-sixth of the population is under 15, and one-sixteenth over 50: the main concentration—76·75 per cent—is between the ages of 15 and 49 years. The

[1] A. G. Sundbärg distinguishes three types of population: the progressive, with a high proportion of children and a high rate of growth; the stationary, with a moderate proportion of children and old persons, and a slow rate of growth, or stationary; and the regressive with a high proportion of old persons and declining numbers. He gives the following modal distribution of ages:

	Under 15 years	15–49	Over 50
Progressive . .	40%	50%	10%
Stationary . .	26·5%	50·5%	23%
Regressive . .	20%	50%	30%

('Sur la répartition de la population par age et sur les taux de mortalité': *Bulletin de l'Internationale de Statistique* (Norway) Tome XX, 1re livraison 1900, pp. 89–94, quoted in 'The Determinants and Consequents of Population Trends: A Summary of the Findings of Studies on the Relationships between Population Changes and Economic and Social Conditions': Department of Social Affairs, Population Division, United Nations, New York, 1953, footnote 45, p. 141, and footnote 66, pp. 141–2.

TABLE XIV

MEDIAN AND QUARTILE AGES BY SEX AND RACE, DURBAN: 1951 CENSUS

AGES IN YEARS

	EUROPEANS			COLOUREDS			INDIANS			AFRICANS		
	Male	Female	Total	Male	Female	Total	Male	Female	Total	Male	Female	Total
First Quartile .	14·77	16·02	15·40	7·17	8·89	7·99	7·25	6·85	7·05	21·13	14·45	19·80
Median . .	30·39	32·45	31·41	17·15	20·22	18·86	16·80	15·56	16·18	28·66	24·77	27·56
Third Quartile .	46·38	49·25	47·86	30·32	33·96	32·39	31·45	28·85	30·06	37·96	34·21	36·93

NOTE.—We excluded from our calculations persons whose ages were shown as 'unspecified' in the Census Tables—save in the case of Africans, where the returns of 'unspecified' numbered only 4.

median age is 27·56, and half the population is in the age range of 19 to 37, that is to say, relatively young adults (Table XIV). The concentration in the working years is more marked for African men than women, as appears clearly from Figure 4. The close parity between the sexes in the group under 15 years is in striking contrast to the dominant male character of the population between the ages of 15 and 49.

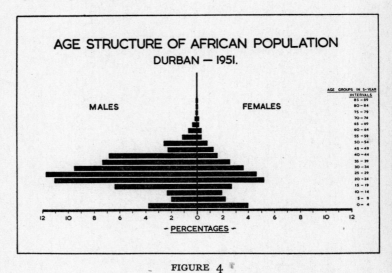

FIGURE 4

AGE STRUCTURE OF THE AFRICAN POPULATION, DURBAN:
1951 CENSUS

Comparisons of the marital status of Africans and of other sections of the population are difficult. The figures for the percentages of Africans married (whether by civil, religious or traditional rites—Table XV), are not very different from those of Europeans, Indians and Coloureds, but our Tables from the Census Department do not show the relatively large numbers of married African men living away from their wives. We cannot make the customary inference that the category of married persons refers to husbands and wives living together, because of the effects of the migratory labour system. Another consequence of migratory labour is the relatively large number of African men and women 'living together', but not married. Only one European, two Coloureds and three Indians are shown as living

TABLE XV

MARITAL STATUS, BY RACE, OF DURBAN'S POPULATION, AGED 15 YEARS AND OVER: 1951 CENSUS

MARITAL STATUS	PERCENTAGES			
	Europeans	*Coloureds*	*Indians*	*Africans*
Never married . .	25·27	41·92	33·81	39·53
Married . . .	63·09	48·29	58·24	51·42*
Widowed . . .	9·03	7·94	7·30	4·03
Divorced . . .	2·59	1·82	0·63	0·54
Living together . .	0·00	0·02	0·00	4·48
Unspecified . . .	0·02	0·01	0·02	0·00
TOTAL . .	100·00	100·00	100·00	100·00

* 22·75 per cent married by civil or religious rites, and 28·67 per cent by traditional (lobola) rites.

together, in comparison with 5,112 Africans (4·48 per cent of the total African population over fifteen years in age). The figures are, of course, unreliable, but indicate that 'living together' is an accepted status among Africans. The percentage of divorced persons (0·54) is the lowest of the four races. In the case of Africans, however, it is not a satisfactory index of the extent of family disorganization, which is more accurately indicated in the number of casual unions.

Fertility rates for Africans in Durban (that is the number of children under 5 years of age to every thousand women in the child-bearing ages of 15–44 inclusive) are also inadequate as an index of reproduction. The lowest rate for the four groups in Durban (385·93), it is widely different from the 1946 African fertility rate of 615·82 for the Union as a whole, indicating the partial picture which the urban statistics give of a migrant population in process of urbanization.

TABLE XVI

FERTILITY RATES, BY RACE, FOR DURBAN, 1951, AND FOR THE UNION OF SOUTH AFRICA, 1946*

RACE	FERTILITY RATES FOR DURBAN	FERTILITY RATES FOR THE UNION OF S.A.	
		Urban	Total
European .	428·72	432·26	488·36
Coloured .	664·48	579·42	697·25
Indian . .	881·40	879·45	901·10
African . .	385·93	379·60	615·82

* Census Data for 1951 are not yet available.

The general unreliability of vital statistics for the African population is particularly marked in the case of birth and death rates. In Figures 5 and 6 we have plotted these rates for the racial groups from data in the Annual Reports of the Medical Officer of Health. Many factors contribute to the jagged fluctuations in our charts. Registration of African births and deaths was inadequate, and, as a result of the close relationship between the city and the reserves— the return to their rural homes of women in pregnancy, and of men and women in sickness—statistics compiled in the city present only an incomplete picture. The increase in birth and death rates over the years expresses not only

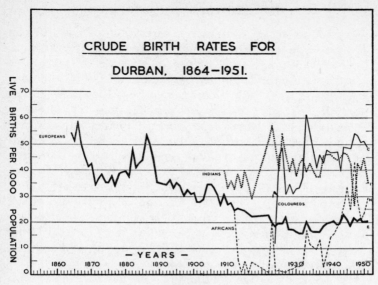

FIGURE 5

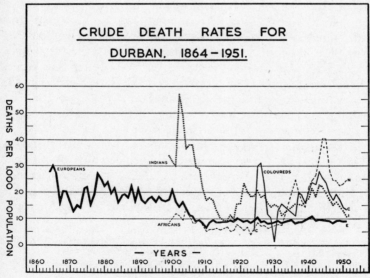

FIGURE 6

changes in the age and sex composition of the African population, but also increasing accuracy in registration. However, even the 1951 figures of a crude death rate of 24·43 per thousand population (the highest of the four groups), and a crude birth rate of 29·51 (lower than Indian and Coloured) may still be very inaccurate.[1]

The Indians of Durban, in contrast to the Africans, are a young population, with a balanced age and sex distribution. Almost half the Indian population (47·52 per cent compared with 16·31 per cent African) is under the age of 15 years, while 45·64 per cent (compared with 76·75 per cent African) is between the age of 15 and 49 years. The percentage over 50 years (6·84) is about the same for Indians as for Africans. The median age of 16·18, the lowest of the four groups (Table XIV, p. 69), explains the high dependency rate among Indians.

The sex distribution of Indians, 104 males to every 100 females (Table XIII, p. 68), corresponds to the biological norm. In the early days there was a high Indian masculinity rate, since no provision was made for women to accompany the indentured men until 1874, and even then agreements with the Government of India stipulated quotas which averaged 30–50 women for every 100 men. Later, as a result of the termination of the indentured labour system in 1911, restrictions on immigration from India in 1913 and the barriers to interprovincial movement, the Indians in Natal became a relatively closed population.

Most of the indentured labourers have now died, and in their place are new generations, the product of natural reproduction, not of immigration. There is some movement of Indians from the rural areas of Natal to Durban; it is not a selective migration of men, as in the case of the Africans,

[1] The Institute of Family and Community Health maintained a reliable system for registration of births and deaths in Lamont Native Township, Durban. This is a township for family units, and very different in composition from the Durban African population as a whole. In 1950–1, birth rates of the Lamont population were 54·4 and death rates 12·6.

but generally a migration of whole families. The combination of anti-Indian sentiment, which rendered the Indians of Natal a closed population, and the solidarity of the Indian family have provided conditions under which the biological forces of birth and death pursue their normal course, undisturbed by such social forces as selective

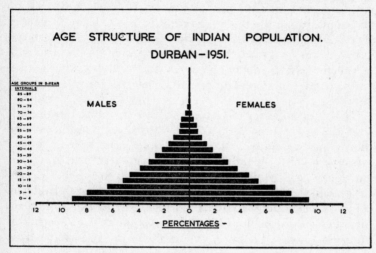

AGE STRUCTURE OF INDIAN POPULATION.
DURBAN – 1951.

FIGURE 7

AGE STRUCTURE OF THE INDIAN POPULATION, DURBAN:
1951 CENSUS

migration. This would explain the normal sex distribution, and the close approximation of the age structure of the Indian population to the theoretical shape of the J curve of population distribution (Figure 7). Not only is there an even distribution of age groups, but the two halves of the pyramid are very symmetrical, save in the age group over 60 years, where the sex ratio is possibly affected by surviving indentured labourers.

The birth and death rates plotted in Figures 5 and 6 (p. 73) are clearly unreliable, and calculations of natural increase based on these figures may be disregarded. The death rate of 10·61, recorded for 1951, is probably fairly accurate, but the figure of 35·32 for the birth rate is doubtful.[1] In the absence of age specific rates, however, we cannot estimate the reproductive capacity of the population. Nor do the Census counts provide a basis, because of the changing age and sex structure, and the more complete enumeration of population in the later, as compared with earlier, Censuses. The fertility rate of 881·40, the highest of the four groups, provides the best available index. A young population, with an even distribution of the sexes and relatively high birth rates, the Indians of Durban may be expected to increase rapidly.

The small number of Coloureds may be related to the fact that the sex composition of the European population was more evenly balanced than we would expect in a pioneer settlement. In 1867, when the municipal census gave the European sex composition for the first time, there were 1,742 males and 1,521 females (a sex ratio of 115 males to every 100 females). No doubt, the 'passing' of Coloureds into the European population has also helped to keep their numbers down. For many years they appear to have been identified with the European population; they were included with Europeans in the Census counts until 1902, and in the statistics of birth and death registrations until 1924.

The general age structure of the Coloured population approximates that of the Indian, a distribution close to the normal J distribution curve (Figure 8). The main irregularity is in the age group 20 to 29 for men, and 15 to 39 for women. It is most improbable that there has been an appreciable decline in birth rates; the 1951 rate was 49 live births per

---

[1] For Indians living in the area of Merebank, Durban, the Institute of Family and Community Health gives the 1951 birth rate as 32·45, and the death rate as 9·49. This is some confirmation of the accuracy of the Indian birth rate of 35·32 for Durban as a whole. On the other hand, the Indian fertility rate is higher than that of Coloureds (see Table XVI, p. 72), and the crude birth rate of Coloureds in 1951 was 49 per 1,000, suggesting then considerable under-registration of Indian births.

1,000 population, and the general trend has been in the direction of an increasing birth rate, though earlier figures are certainly unreliable. Hence the bulge in the population pyramid at the ages of able-bodied workers is probably due to migration, more particularly of women. The sex ratio fell from 0·98 in 1946 to 0·88 in 1951,[1] suggesting a greater influx of Coloured women than of Coloured men in recent years.

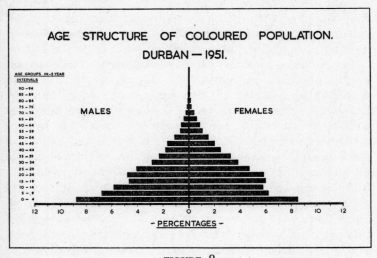

FIGURE 8

AGE STRUCTURE OF THE COLOURED POPULATION, DURBAN:
1951 CENSUS

The Coloureds are a young population, with 41·80 per cent under the age of 15 (as compared with 47·52 per cent Indians), 50·15 per cent between the ages of 15 and 49 years (Indians 45·64 per cent) and 8·05 per cent over the age of 50 years (Indians 6·84 per cent). The median age is 18·86, about 2½ years above the median age for Indians and more

[1] The main towns in the Union had Coloured sex ratios below unity in 1946. We can offer no explanation for what appears to be a large migration of Coloured women into Durban between 1946 and 1951.

than 12 years below the European. Half the Coloured population is between the ages of 8 and 33 (Table XIV, p. 69). Fertility rates for the Coloureds are 664·48, appreciably above the European and African rates (Table XVI, p. 72). With a young population, high birth rates and a declining death rate, the Coloureds are clearly on the threshold of rapid population increase. The current classification of all persons in race categories, under the Population Registration Act, No. 30 of 1950, will have the effect of accelerating this increase, since a proportion of the Coloureds who had passed into the European population will be returned to the fold.

This will also have the effect of reducing to a small extent the numbers of Europeans, an ageing population with declining birth rates. It is appreciably older than the European urban population as a whole; in 1946 there was a difference in median age of almost five years. The present median age of 31·41 (Table XIV, p. 69) is the highest of the four racial groups in Durban and almost double that of the Indians. About one-quarter of the European population is under the age of 15 years as compared with almost half the Indian population, while in the age range of over 50 years there are 22·22 per cent of Europeans as against 6·84 per cent Indians. The age pyramid shown in Figure 9 is very narrowly based, as compared with the Indian and Coloured, while the relatively high proportions in the age categories over 20 years of age reflect the influence of declining birth and death rates, and of migration.

In contrast to the Indian and African populations, Europeans and Coloureds have more women than men (Table XIII, p. 68). From 1867 the European sex ratio remained fairly constant, apart from fluctuations probably associated with the presence of troops in the city. It is only during the period of the world wars and industrialization that the ratio falls below parity to the 1951 level of 0·95. The general trend to increasing femininity is a characteristic of the city population as a whole and of each of its races.

The median age of European and Coloured women is higher than that of European and Coloured men respectively (Table XIV, p. 69). This is the normal pattern, since women generally have a longer expectation of life than men. It contrasts, however, with the younger average age of African and Indian women when compared with men. The cause,

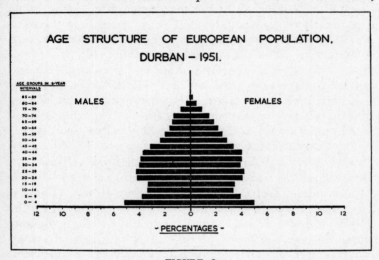

FIGURE 9

AGE STRUCTURE OF THE EUROPEAN POPULATION, DURBAN: 1951 CENSUS

in the case of Africans, is the selective migration of adult men, while in the case of Indians an explanation is generally found in the assumed survival of an older generation of men who came under the indentured system. This may be a factor, but the real cause appears to be the higher survival rate of Indian men.

The marital status of Europeans differs markedly from that of other groups in Durban. Europeans have the highest proportions married, widowed, and divorced (Table XV, p. 71). Precise comparisons cannot be made on the basis of our Tables, which give marital status for the population over 15 years of age, because of the very different age structure of the groups. We would expect the Europeans to have a higher proportion of married persons since they are an older population. This may also affect the proportion of divorced persons: the European population has twice as many divorced persons as the three remaining groups taken together. The divorce rate, that is the number of divorced persons per 1,000 married persons, gives a better basis for comparison. It is highest for Europeans and Coloureds (41·1 and 37·7) and low for Indians and Africans (10·9 and 10·5). The young population of Coloureds thus shows the same readiness to divorce as the Europeans, while among Indians divorce is certainly uncommon: in the African population its incidence is no doubt masked by casual unions.

The widowed rate for Europeans is 143·1 per 1,000 married persons, which is lower than the Coloured (164·5) and higher than the Indian (125·4) and African (72·11). The African rate is thus the lowest of the four groups. There is a preponderance in each race of widows to widowers: the African rate for widows is not very different from the rate for Europeans, Indians and Coloureds. African widowers, however, are a relatively small proportion of survivors. Presumably, then, African men remarry or establish casual unions more readily.

Vital statistics for Europeans are relatively reliable. Birth rates (Figure 5, p. 73) have declined steadily—though with fluctuations as, for example, during the period of the Second World War—to the figure of 20·54 live births per 1,000 population (average for 1949–51). Similarly, death rates declined until 1910,[1] and from that date have remained

---

[1] The Medical Officer of Health for Durban attributed the fall in death rates during the preceding few years to improvements in sanitation and the draining of swamps (Annual Mayor's Minute, 1910). The European death rate in the Union as a whole, for the three years 1949–51, is 8·8 deaths per 1,000 population, compared with a rate of 9·20 for Durban, a difference attributable, in part, to an older age structure in Durban.

relatively stationary at under 10 deaths per 1,000 population (Figure 6, p. 73). The fertility rates of 428·72 are higher than those of Africans, but considerably lower than Coloured and Indian (Table XVI, p. 72). Comparisons are, however, not valid in the case of Africans, because of the incomplete picture presented by statistics for a migrant population, analysed in isolation from its rural base. The Europeans of Durban, with declining birth rates and a high proportion of old people, are a relatively stationary or indeed regressive population. In contrast to the Indian and Coloured populations, where rapid increase may be expected as a result of reproductive forces, any large European increase is dependent on migration from other provinces or from overseas.

The European population is indeed already a population swelled by migrants. Only 42·40 per cent of Europeans were born in Natal. This percentage understates the extent of migration, since it takes no account of movement from other areas of Natal to Durban, information not supplied to us by the Census Department. Migration is probably selective not only of European adults of working age, but also of old, retired, widowed and divorced persons, drawn to Durban by its attraction as a comfortable seaside resort.

Using birth within Natal as an index of the extent to which a population is indigenous, the races are ranked in the following order: Indians (94·68 per cent), Africans (86·84 per cent), Coloureds (76·69 per cent) and Europeans (42·40 per cent). Less than 5 per cent of Durban Indians were born outside South Africa and less than 1 per cent in provinces other than Natal, as compared with 25 per cent of Europeans born outside South Africa and over 32 per cent in other provinces. The recruitment of Africans and Coloureds from outside South Africa is small, and only the Cape, among the other provinces of South Africa, has contributed appreciably to their numbers.

F

TABLE XVII

BIRTHPLACE OF DURBAN POPULATION:
1951 CENSUS

Place of Birth	Europeans	Coloureds	Indians	Africans	Total
Cape Province .	14·70	16·72	0·16	8·72	7·95
Natal . .	42·40	76·69	94·68	86·84	75·55
Transvaal . .	13·39	3·43	0·37	1·24	4·74
Orange Free State	4·24	1·13	0·01	1·00	1·66
South Africa .	0·34	0·14	0·12	0·02	0·15
Total for Union	75·07	98·11	95·34	97·82	90·05
Rest of Africa* .	1·99	1·61	0·11	2·17	1·39
United Kingdom	17·16	0·04	0·01	0·00	5·24
Rest of World .	5·78	0·24	4·54	0·01	3·32
Total . .	100·00	100·00	100·00	100·00	100·00
Total for Africa .	77·06	99·72	95·45	99·99	91·44
Overseas Total .	22·94	0·28	4·55	0·01	8·56

* Includes St Helena, Mauritius, Madagascar.

Adding to the complexity of racial differences are the wide variations within each racial group in occupation and income, as we have already seen, and also in religion and language. Differences in the life chances of the individual are associated with home language and religious affiliation.

The wide range of religious affiliation is shown opposite. The broad difference in religious affiliation is between the Indians and the other races. Indians are predominantly Hindu (73·87 per cent) and Muslim (16·03 per cent), while Europeans, Coloureds and Africans are predominantly Christian (95·65 per cent, 91·96 per cent and 90·28 per cent respectively). The Jewish population is small, 3·27 per cent of the total European.

The major differences in the Christian population are in

TABLE XVIII

RELIGIOUS AFFILIATION OF THE POPULATION OF DURBAN, BY RACE: 1951 CENSUS

RELIGIOUS GROUP	Europeans	Coloureds	Indians	Africans
CHRISTIAN SECTS				
Afrikaans Protestant .	12·83	0·90	0·01	0·81
Anglican . . .	28·60	24·18	0·74	8·34
Other Protestant . .	36·21	14·17	1·34	20·55
Roman Catholic . .	12·07	43·59	1·47	15·91
Minor Sects . . .	5·94	9·12	3·12	44·67
TOTAL—Christian .	95·65	91·96	6·68	90·28
Jewish	3·27	0·04	0·00	0·00
ORIENTAL AND ISLAMIC				
Buddhist . . .	0·00	—	0·13	0·00
Confucian . . .	—	—	0·02	—
Hindu	0·01	1·11	73·87	0·01
Islamic . . .	0·01	5·78	16·03	0·25
Parsee . . .	—	—	0·02	0·00
TOTAL—Oriental and Islamic	0·02	6·89	90·07	0·26
Quasi-Religious, No Religion, Unspecified . .	1·06	1·11	3·25	9·46
TOTAL	100·00	100·00	100·00	100·00

NOTE 1.—The religious denominations in each category are as follows: *Afrikaans Protestant*—De Vos Kerke, Nederduitse Gereformeerde/ Hervormde Kerk, Gereformeerde Kerke—Dopper Kerk, Nederduits Hervormde Kerk. *Other Protestant (excluding Anglican)*—Church of England in South Africa, Presbyterian, Congregationalist, Methodist, Lutheran, Baptist. *Minor Sects*—Greek Church (included under this heading because very small numbers are involved), Christian Scientist, Plymouth Brethren, Salvation Army, Seventh Day Adventist, Apostolic Faith Mission Church, Full Gospel Church (of God) Gospel Mission, African Separatist Churches, Apostolic Sects, other Minor Sects. 'The Church of England in South Africa' has a large membership—8·54 per cent of Europeans, and 4·18 per cent of Coloureds. It seems probable that the majority of persons in this category should be classified as Anglican, and not under the heading 'Other Protestant'. This would raise the Anglican membership to about 35 per cent of Europeans.

NOTE 2.—We have included, in the Indian group, the 73 Chinese-speaking persons who live in Durban.

the strength of minor sects[1] among the Africans and of Catholicism among the Coloureds. Almost half the African population belongs to minor sects, which have in general, as we would expect, a greater appeal for Non-European than European Christians. So, too, the Roman Catholic Church has a relatively higher membership among Non-European than European Christians. This is especially marked in the case of Coloureds, with over 43 per cent Roman Catholic as compared with 12·07 per cent of Europeans. In contrast, the Afrikaans Protestant Churches, with a larger European membership than the Roman Catholic Church (12·83 per cent), have a membership of less than 1 per cent Coloureds and Africans, and 0·01 per cent Indians.

The languages are as diverse as the religions. Europeans and Coloureds are predominantly English-speaking (83·63 per cent Europeans and 81·98 per cent Coloureds), though an appreciable proportion speaks Afrikaans (13·11 per cent Europeans and 12·43 per cent Coloureds). Since most of the Afrikaans-speaking Europeans belong to one or other of the Afrikaans Protestant Churches (12·83 per cent of Europeans are affiliated), the low membership of 0·90 per cent of Coloureds in these Churches is of considerable interest. For the rest, small numbers of Europeans and Coloureds speak both English and Afrikaans, or one of a large number of European languages.

Durban has a very high proportion of English-speaking Europeans. At the time of the 1946 Census[2] the proportion of English-speaking inhabitants of the five largest cities was as follows: Johannesburg, 64·72 per cent; Cape Town, 74·91 per cent; Port Elizabeth, 58·98 per cent; Durban, 85·09 per cent; and the capital, Pretoria, 36·87 per cent. However, the Afrikaans population has been moving slowly

[1] These minor sects include the African Separatist Churches, many of which combine Christian observance with elements of African belief and ritual.
[2] Vol. IV, 1946 Census Report: *Languages and Literacy* (U.G. 18/1954, pp. 80–1).

into Durban.[1] We may expect this process to accelerate. Some three-fifths of the entire European population of South Africa speaks Afrikaans, urbanization of the European population is mainly an urbanization of the rural Afrikaner, and the Afrikaners have a much higher rate of reproduction

TABLE XIX

HOME LANGUAGES OF EUROPEANS AND COLOUREDS, DURBAN: 1951 CENSUS

HOME LANGUAGE	NUMBERS		PERCENTAGES	
	Europeans	Coloureds	Europeans	Coloureds
English & Afrikaans	1,768	311	1·35	1·89
English	109,782	13,518	83·63	81·98
Afrikaans	17,217	2,050	13·11	12·43
Dutch	550	21	0·42	0·13
German	330	61	0·25	0·37
Yiddish/Hebrew	147	6	0·11	0·04
Greek	92	15	0·07	0·09
Italian	149	91	0·11	0·55
Portuguese	84	27	0·06	0·16
French	675	179	0·51	1·09
Unspecified	17	18	0·01	0·11
Other	482	192	0·37	1·16
TOTAL	131,293	16,489	100·00	100·00

than the English. With this changing language structure of the European population of Durban, and a large recruitment of population, as we have already seen, from other provinces of the Union, the political outlook of the Durban

---

[1] The term 'Dutch', not 'Afrikaans', was used in the 1921 Census. In the 1926 Census the words 'Dutch' and 'Afrikaans' were being used interchangeably. It was only from 1936 that the Census provided information as to home language: previously, the information related to the ability to *speak* one or both of the official languages. The percentage of Europeans in Durban with Afrikaans as home language was 8·09 per cent in 1936 and 13·11 per cent in 1951.

voter is certain to be transformed, as Durban ceases to be a centre of British sentiment.

The Indian population has a more varied language structure than the European and Coloured. The main language groups are Tamil (37·72 per cent), Hindi (25·37

TABLE XX

HOME LANGUAGES OF INDIANS,*
DURBAN: 1951 CENSUS

Home Language	Numbers	Percentage
English and Afrikaans .	19	0·01
English	8,342	5·71
Afrikaans . . .	27	0·02
Tamil	55,140	37·72
Hindi	37,088	25·37
Telugu	17,075	11·68
Gujarati	8,776	6·00
Urdu	13,617	9·32
Other Indian . . .	5,729	3·92
Chinese	73	0·05
Other Languages . .	194	0·13
Unspecified . . .	103	0·07
TOTAL . .	146,183	100·00

* Again, we have not separated out the 73 Chinese-speaking.

per cent), Telugu (11·68 per cent), Urdu (9·32 per cent), Gujarati (6·00 per cent) and English (5·71 per cent). Only a negligible proportion speak Afrikaans. Most Indians know some English, and increasingly English is becoming their home language, though fear that their children will be ignorant of the traditional Indian languages, and probably also the challenge of Christianity, have led to some development of vernacular schools.

Most Africans speak Zulu as their home language (86·30

per cent) or allied Nguni languages (Xhosa, 7·46 per cent; Swazi, 1·19 per cent; and Ndebele, 0·07 per cent). Zulu is the *lingua franca* of the African population of Durban. Few give English and Afrikaans as home languages: many are, however, familiar with English.

TABLE XXI

HOME LANGUAGES OF AFRICANS, DURBAN: 1951 CENSUS

HOME LANGUAGE	NUMBERS	PERCENTAGE
Xhosa	10,148	7·46
Zulu	117,601	86·30
Swazi	1,626	1·19
Ndebele	97	0·07
South-Sotho . . .	4,885	3·58
Sechuana . . .	192	0·14
Sepedi	315	0·23
Shangaan . . .	346	0·25
Venda	45	0·03
English	58	0·04
Afrikaans . . .	48	0·04
Other and Unspecified .	918	0·67
TOTAL . .	136,279	100·00

The relationship between the home languages of Europeans, Coloureds and Indians, and their life chances, as measured by mean and *per capita* income, is shown in Table XXII.[1] Comparable data are not available for Africans.

The first distinction, over-riding home language, is that between European and Non-European. Only the Chinese-speaking (numbering 73 all told) and the Gujarati (6 per

[1] We have not included the full Table of Income Distribution by Home Language. This Table, and most of our original Tables from the Census Department, are reproduced in 'An Urban Morphology of Durban', a thesis submitted by Mrs M. A. Tatham in 1954 for the degree of Master of Arts at the University of Natal.

cent of the Indian population) receive incomes comparable
with those of Europeans. However, both have higher
dependency rates, reducing their *per capita* incomes well
below the average European *per capita* income. For the
rest, not one of the Non-European language groups earns
much more than half the income of any of the European
language groups, while *per capita* income varies from about
one-sixth to a little over a third of the *per capita* income of
the poorest European language group.

The favoured language groups among the earning
population of Europeans and Coloureds are the same: first,
the foreign language group; then the English, followed
by those whose home languages are English and Afrikaans;
and finally the Afrikaans-speaking. The English-speaking
Europeans have the lowest dependency rate and the highest
per capita income, while the Afrikaans-speaking Europeans
have the highest dependency rate and very much the lowest
per capita income. In the case of Afrikaans-speaking women,
the dependency rate is particularly high, indicating that
they enter into employment less readily than other groups.
The range in *per capita* income is wide, from £298·93 for
the English-speaking to £185·04 for the Afrikaans-speaking.
There is thus the expected relationship between income and
dependants—those with the smallest income have most
dependants.

This relationship, however, is not found among the
Coloureds where the groups with the highest earning
capacity have most dependants. The effect is to level *per
capita* income. Afrikaans-speaking Coloureds earn least but
have the lowest dependency rate, with the result that their
per capita income (£60·22) is very little below that of the
foreign-speaking, who have both the highest income and the
highest dependency rates.

Inequality in mean income is most marked among the
Indian language groups, ranging from £458·42 for the
Gujarati to £144·95 for the Telugu. Since all the groups

have high dependency rates, the inequality is reflected also in *per capita* income, though the range is much narrower—from £102·71 for the Gujarati to £33·25 for the Telugu and £32·19 for the Tamil. The English-speaking Indians have

TABLE XXII

HOME LANGUAGE, ANNUAL MEAN INCOME,*
DEPENDENCY RATE† AND *PER CAPITA* INCOME,
DURBAN: 1951 CENSUS

(*a*) EUROPEANS

Home Language	Mean Income	Dependency Rate			Per Capita Income
		Male	*Female*	*Total*	
Foreign ‡ . .	£597·73	43·01	287·96	110·55	£284·14
English . . .	£571·76	43·60	174·40	91·27	£298·93
English and Afrikaans	£450·79	40·19	235·74	98·31	£227·32
Afrikaans . .	£410·78	51·38	380·40	121·99	£185·04
Total . .	£552·06	44·62	191·52	95·25	£282·74

(*b*) COLOUREDS

Home Language	Mean Income	Dependency Rate			Per Capita Income
		Male	*Female*	*Total*	
Foreign . . .	£215·18	152·94	396·97	248·81	£61·69
English . . .	£212·24	160·67	318·41	226·89	£64·93
English and Afrikaans	£184·84	100·00	260·98	154·10	£72·74
Afrikaans . .	£146·22	94·18	221·14	142·81	£60·22
Total . .	£201·20	147·98	305·45	212·72	£64·34

* Of persons in receipt of income.
† Number of persons *not* in receipt of income per 100 persons in receipt of income.
‡ Languages other than English and Afrikaans—see Table XIX, p. 85.

(c) INDIANS §

Home Language	Mean Income	Dependency Rate			Per Capita Income
		Male	Female	Total	
Chinese . .	£563·46	126·32	328·57	180·77	£200·68
Gujarati . .	£458·42	147·07	2,761·07	346·29	£102·71
English . .	£219·23	120·36	1,022·22	239·82	£64·51
Urdu . . .	£208·91	187·09	4,709·92	441·87	£38·55
Hindi . . .	£165·06	162·18	3,339·43	382·05	£34·24
Tamil . . .	£146·09	152·57	2,218·76	353·73	£32·19
Telugu . .	£144·95	147·57	1,916·39	335·99	£33·25
Total . .	£182·85	154·88	2,404·30	356·85	£40·02

§ Includes 73 Chinese-speaking.

the lowest dependency rate both for men and women, indicating a westernization already expressed in the adoption of English as their home language. Among the more prosperous Gujarati very few women work, as is true also of Hindi, and to a lesser extent, Tamil and Telugu.[1] Most conservative of all, in the non-employment of women outside the home, are the Urdu-speaking Indians. Although they earn appreciably more than the Telugu, their *per capita* income is very little higher. Tamil, Telugu, Hindi and Urdu (that is 84 per cent or over 120,000 of the Indian population) have a *per capita* income of between £32 and £39 per annum. Only the Gujarati are more favoured than the Coloureds, while the English-speaking Indians are at about the same economic level.

The religious affiliations of the European, Coloured and Indian populations are also associated with inequalities in income (Table XXIII).

Among Europeans there is a wide difference in mean income between Jews and Christians (£1,394·78 for the

[1] Precise comparison is difficult, since there may be differences in age structure.

Jewish group as compared with £549·73 for Anglicans, or £449·17 for Roman Catholics). Although the Jewish group has a relatively high dependency rate, its *per capita* income is still more than double that of the Christian denominations. Of the latter, the denominational categories in receipt of the lowest income, that is the Afrikaans Protestant and the Roman Catholic, have the highest dependency rates. This is the same relationship that we found between the European language groups and income.

Again, as in the case of language groups, this relationship does not hold for the Coloureds. The Muslims receive the highest income but also have the highest dependency rate (apart from the small Coloured Hindu group), and in consequence a lower *per capita* income than members of the Roman Catholic or Protestant Churches. Among the

TABLE XXIII

RELIGION, ANNUAL MEAN INCOME, DEPENDENCY RATE AND *PER CAPITA* INCOME, DURBAN: 1951 CENSUS

(a) EUROPEANS

Religion	Mean Income	Dependency Rate			Per Capita Income
		Male	Female	Total	
Jewish . . .	£1,394·78	41·15	252·14	98·24	£703·56
Indeterminate, None, or Unspecified .	£605·87	24·76	170·56	61·38	£375·42
Protestant (other than Anglican and Afrikaans) . .	£555·20	42·49	174·67	90·39	£291·77
Anglican . .	£549·73	42·07	161·53	86·86	£294·22
Minor Christian Sects	£508·43	49·04	219·30	104·45	£248·68
Roman Catholic .	£449·17	58·64	208·98	115·02	£208·89
Afrikaans Protestant	£428·05	45·92	339·79	112·20	£201·72
Total . .	£552·06	44·62	191·52	95·25	£282·74

(b) COLOUREDS

RELIGION	MEAN INCOME	DEPENDENCY RATE			Per Capita INCOME
		Male	*Female*	*Total*	
Muslim . .	£247·48	195·21	618·06	334·86	£56·91
Anglican . .	£208·52	125·40	278·15	188·18	£72·36
Roman Catholic.	£203·07	170·56	314·87	231·01	£61·35
Protestant (other than Anglican and Afrikaans)	£192·80	110·45	237·50	163·89	£73·06
Minor Christian Sects . .	£180·34	140·21	340·66	218·16	£56·68
Afrikaans Protestant . .	£154·92	123·53	125·00	124·24	£69·09
Indeterminate, None, or Un-specified .	£134·72	155·88	330·00	220·37	£42·05
Hindu* . .	£128·13	688·88	1,500·00	1,043·75	£11·20
TOTAL .	£201·20	147·98	305·50	212·72	£64·34

* Only 71 all told.

(c) INDIANS

RELIGION	MEAN INCOME	DEPENDENCY RATE			Per Capita INCOME
		Male	*Female*	*Total*	
Confucian . .	£859·09	112·50	200·00	136·36	£363·46
Parsee . . .	£321·86	50·00	—*	212·50	£103·00
Muslim . .	£281·72	169·99	3,307·65	397·69	£56·61
Roman Catholic .	£188·11	151·51	624·14	270·49	£50·77
Protestant (excluding Anglican) .	£184·80	146·10	1,030·00	283·14	£48·47
Anglican . .	£167·07	133·06	631·43	244·87	£48·44
Hindu . .	£165·16	153·18	2,579·93	356·79	£36·16
Indeterminate, None, or Unspeci-fied . .	£162·55	145·21	2,157·43	331·32	£37·69
Buddhist . .	£160·33	166·67	1,214·29	326·09	£37·63
Minor Christian Sects .	£150·89	146·34	1,518·71	325·21	£35·41
TOTAL .	£182·85	154·88	2,404·30	356·85	£40·02

* No females in receipt of income in this category.

Christian denominations, the Roman Catholic Coloureds have the highest dependency rate, as is the case also with Europeans, but in contrast to European Catholics, they receive relatively high incomes.

Within the Indian group there is again a wide difference in the dependency rates for Muslims and Hindus on the one hand, and for Catholics, Anglicans and other Protestants on the other. The rates for the latter, as for Indians speaking English, are appreciably lower than those of other Indians, but very much higher than the European rates. This is largely due to differences in age structure between the racial groups, but also indicates an absorption, with Christianity, of European employment patterns, restrained however by the traditional purdah for women. Members of the minor Christian sects, however, retain very high dependency rates. The most economically favoured religion among the Indians is the Parsee, which has a small following in Durban. Next come the Muslims, with relatively high incomes and high dependency rates. Of the Christians, the Roman Catholics have the highest mean and *per capita* income, and members of the minor Christian sects the lowest, while the combination of low income and high dependency rates reduces the *per capita* income of the Hindus, the vast majority of the Indian population, to the impoverished level of £3 per month.

These demographic contrasts between and within the racial groups by no means exhaust the variety and complexity of the population of Durban. We have made no reference to the caste system within the Indian group, still operative in the choice of husband or wife,[1] and sometimes relevant to prestige and to occupation. We have not discussed the wide differences in degree of adjustment to European life, so apparent in the clothing of African and Indian women— tribal costumes, saris, or western dress. Nor have we mentioned the more subtle nuances of an emerging class structure

[1] See Hilda Kuper, 'Changes in Caste of the South African Indians', *Race Relations Journal*, vol. XXII, No. 4, 1955, pp. 18–25.

among the Non-Europeans, nor the more obvious class differences within the European group. And yet the spatial distribution of the population, for all its diversity, is clearly defined, partly as a result of the policies which we examined in the first chapter, and partly as a result of selective social forces.

CHAPTER IV

RESIDENTIAL ECOLOGY
OF THE RACES

The residential ecology of Durban is briefly discussed by
Dr H. C. Brookfield and Mrs A. Tatham in the 'Distribution
of Racial Groups in Durban', *The Geographical Review*,
vol. XLVII, no. 1, 1957, pp. 44–65.
We refer only generally to land usage, which will be fully
discussed in a separate study by Ronald Davies. Our main
concern is with the racial character of residential settlement in
Durban, and we are using the term ecology in the narrow sense
of the spatial distribution of the residents.

THE city and port of Durban lie on the south-eastern
coast of Southern Africa in latitude 29°50' South.
The relatively smooth coastline stretching northwards
from East London is interrupted by the seaward-jutting land
spits of the Bluff and the Point, which enclose the expansive
bay of Durban. The city has grown around the bay, and
now covers some 70 square miles, following the coast and
bay for 16 miles, from the old course of the Umlaas River
in the south to beyond the Umgeni River to the north, and
stretching inland in a broad irregular arc, with a maximum
range from east to west of some 7 miles (Figure 10, p. 96).

Enclosed within these boundaries is an area of varied
relief, with a moderate range of altitude rising from sea-level
on the east to a height of 500–600 feet on the inland margins
of the city. On the basis of relief and geological structure,
we can distinguish five physiographic regions—the Bluff, the
Alluvial Flats, the Berea Ridge, the Inland Hilly Region,
and the Umbilo-Umhlatuzana Interfluve. Each of these has
a significant relationship to the social ecology of the city
(Figure 11).

95

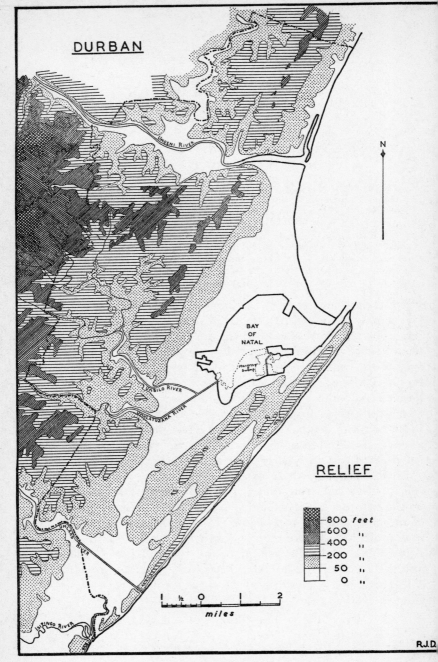

DURBAN

N

BAY
OF
NATAL

Mangrove
Swamp

UMGENI RIVER

UMBILO RIVER

MHLATUZANA RIVER

RIVER

RELIEF

800 feet
600 ''
400 ''
200 ''
50 ''
0 ''

ISIPINGO RIVER

1 ½ O   1   2
miles

R.J.D.

FIGURE 10

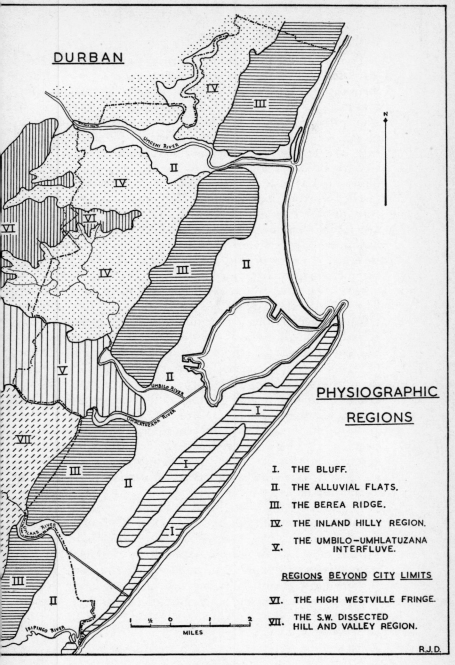

DURBAN

PHYSIOGRAPHIC
REGIONS

I. THE BLUFF.

II. THE ALLUVIAL FLATS.

III. THE BEREA RIDGE.

IV. THE INLAND HILLY REGION.

V. THE UMBILO—UMHLATUZANA
INTERFLUVE.

REGIONS BEYOND CITY LIMITS

VI. THE HIGH WESTVILLE FRINGE.

VII. THE S.W. DISSECTED
HILL AND VALLEY REGION.

MILES

R.J.D.

FIGURE II

G

The Bluff is used mainly for residential and defence purposes. It consists of two narrow parallel ridges, separated for most of their length by a marshy and ill-drained valley, and merging into a single ridge in the north-east (Region I, Figure 11). The Ocean Ridge, with a maximum elevation of 250–300 feet, shelves steeply down to the sea on the one side, and to the valley on the other, while the Bay Ridge, slightly broader, lower and with more moderate slopes, flanks the Bay and the Alluvial Flats, to the west.

The Alluvial Flats (Region II) contain the commercial core of the city and the main industrial zones. These are located around the northern and western shores of the bay and extend southwards towards the Umlaas River. Residential development, separate from the industrial and commercial or intermingled with it, ranges from the poorest of shack settlements to modern luxury flats on the bay front. The Alluvial Flats stretch southwards from the banks of the Umgeni River to the Umbogintwini River, beyond the city boundaries, and occupy a considerable tract of land between the foot of the Berea Ridge and the sea, the bay shores and the Bluff. They consist essentially of alluvial material deposited by the main rivers in the area, the Umgeni, Umbilo, Umhlatuzana, Umlaas, Isipingo and Umbogintwini, and vary in width from one to three miles. Altitude rarely exceeds 40 feet, and the flats were subject to periodic flooding in the past: even in the two main streets, hollows became impassable swamps after rains. Smaller but important alluvial flats along the river banks are used for market gardening by Indian families.

The Berea Ridge (III), like the Bluff, is mainly an area of residential development. Though a continuous feature trending NNE to SSW across the centre of the borough, and broken only by the narrow gaps cut by the rivers, it falls into three well-defined sections. The northern section beyond the Umgeni River has a distinctive character, since it rises directly from the sea, while the central and southern sections of the ridge are separated from the sea by the Alluvial Flats, with their commercial and industrial development, and by the Bay and the Bluff. So, too, the southern section of the ridge is differentiated by the fact that it merges with the Inland Hilly Region, whereas the central and northern portions are most clearly defined and sharply separated from the inland hills by streams draining northwards and southwards. And finally, the central ridge, between the Umgeni and Umbilo Rivers, has unique characteristics as an area of long settlement falling within the Old Borough, and flanking the city centre.

The northern and central sections of the ridge are particularly attractive for residential settlement, with a relatively high elevation between 400 and 500 feet, and present a fairly uniform, gently sloping surface to the sea, indented at intervals by well-marked drainage lines leading to the Alluvial Flats below. The southern section of the ridge is less attractive, since it is cut off from the sea by the Bluff.

The Inland Hilly Region (IV), an area of complicated relief, geology and drainage, occupies a large tract of land between the Central Berea Ridge and the city boundaries to the west. Elevated hills and ridges reach a height of 300–400 feet, and the Umgeni and Umbilo watershed a height of over 500 feet. Much of the area is undeveloped; residential settlements include housing estates, the Cato Manor slums, modest owner-built houses, and some good-quality housing, especially in the region of the watershed. To the west the region gives way to more elevated ridges at Westville (VI) and beyond, reaching altitudes of over 1,000 feet, and providing favourable sites for a number of small towns, which serve also as dormitory suburbs for Durban.

The Umbilo-Umhlatuzana Interfluve (V), mainly residential in character, takes the form of a ridge, trending east-west rather than north-south, as do the other relief features. It reaches a maximum height of 400–450 feet on the western boundaries, and has a partial seaward-facing

aspect. From the narrow crest of the ridge, the land slopes fairly steeply down into the two river valleys. The interfluve itself is dissected by drainage lines and assumes an irregular and hilly nature for the most part.

Seaward aspect and elevation above sea level are major factors in the distribution of the population of Durban. This is, no doubt, partly for aesthetic reasons, but also because of climate, which is sub-tropical and unusually warm for latitude 30° S. Durban's mild dry winter climate is the city's greatest asset as a holiday resort, providing ideal physical conditions for human comfort. The average temperature for the coolest month is 64·3° Fahrenheit, while night temperatures seldom fall below 50° Fahrenheit on the seaward side of the Berea Ridge, though light frosts occur in the valleys behind. Summers, on the other hand, are long, hot and very humid, and the slight variations in the daily range of temperature afford little relief from the incessant enervating heat and humidity. This summer discomfort is less acute at the higher elevations above sea level, and on the seaward-facing slopes. The sea breeze, in particular, plays an important part in tempering summer heat and humidity; it is strongly felt on the Sea Front, the Berea Ridge, and the Ocean Ridge of the Bluff, but to a limited degree only in the Alluvial Flats, and in the Inland Hilly Region below altitudes of about 500 feet.

The influence of these factors on Europeans is clear in newspaper advertisements of homes for sale. There is an emphasis on such topographical features as height above sea level, seaward aspect and view, phrased as 'commanding position on the Berea', 'view site', or 'panoramic view'. 'High position' or 'good views' suggests that the property is not very high up on the Berea, and 'fine inland views' is an attempt to compensate for a less desirable site. With increasing pressure on the small area of seaward-facing slopes, more and more Europeans are obliged to appreciate the aesthetic satisfactions of the inland site.

Among the Non-European groups, only the Indians were in any way competitors for the available land, and even this competition was severely limited by the general impoverishment of the Indian population. Very few could have hoped for fine homes on the Berea, and the possession of such homes was not so necessary a mark of social prestige. In recent years the 'pegging' Acts, which froze the *status quo* and restricted the play of the property market, effectively blocked the expression of ecological competition. Today the problem for Indians under the Group Areas Act is largely that of availability, rather than desirability.[1]

The effect of topography and climate on racial distribution and property values is demonstrated, in a general way, by the profiles in Figure 12 (pp. 102, 103, 104). We drew six lines across the city and traced, along their course, race composition, rateable value and height.[2] At the left of each profile is the sea; the wavy line on the vertical axis represents altitude, the vertical bars indicate rateable values, while the hatchings on the horizontal plane gives the percentage of Europeans. Commercial and industrial areas, the University, schools, parks, railways, hotels, flats, boarding houses, the port and harbour installations are left blank.

Thus, in profile (1), the high peaks in terms of altitude, rateable value, and proportion European, fall on the Ocean Ridge (Brighton Beach) and the Bay Ridge (Wentworth) of the Bluff. Between these ridges lies a sparsely inhabited valley. To the right from Wentworth we move on to the

[1] Similar standards of desirability to those of European residents operate among sections of the Indian population. For example, in a letter to the Secretary of the Lawrence Committee, dated 13th July 1942, the Natal Indian Association stated that Indians had moved into European areas because the City Council denied them sites with 'commanding' views and possessing all the civic amenities.

[2] Dr H. C. Brookfield suggested this technique. Rateable values for residential buildings, excluding flats, hotels and boarding-houses, were extracted from the municipal valuation roll for 1951: race composition is based on the 1951 Census count in each of the enumerators' sub-districts through which the cross-sections pass. The cross-sections were drawn on a map of the city from selected points on the coastline to the inland areas, in such a way as to traverse the major topographical features of the city.

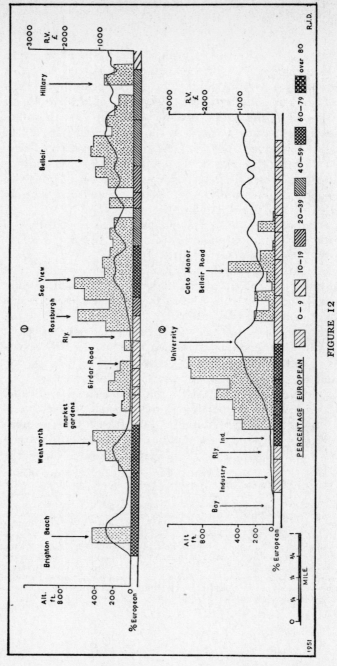

FIGURE I2

VERTICAL PROFILES ACROSS DURBAN, RELATING RELIEF, MUNICIPAL VALUATION OF RESIDENTIAL PROPERTIES,
AND RACIAL COMPOSITION

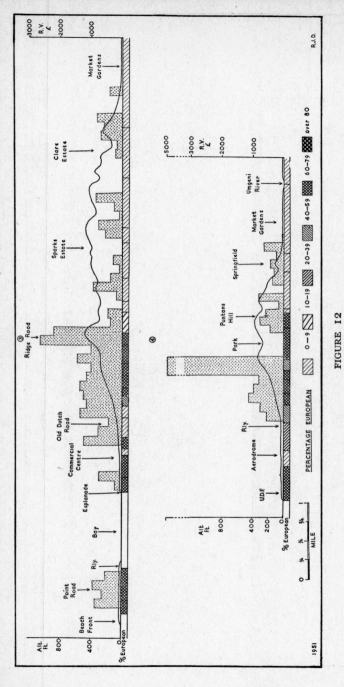

FIGURE 12

VERTICAL PROFILES—CONTINUED

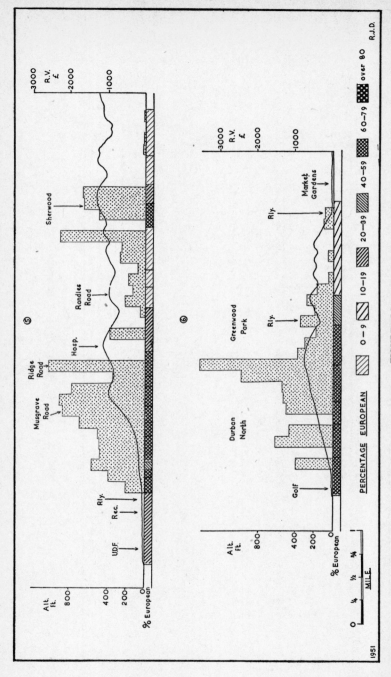

FIGURE 12

VERTICAL PROFILES—CONTINUED

low-lying Alluvial Flats, which are also a trough in rateable values and predominantly Non-European. Then the ground rises in the Umbilo-Umhlatuzana Interfluve, attaining the highest rateable value and the maximum European concentration at Sea View. Non-Europeans are, however, well established throughout the interfluve, which is relatively high and has a partially seaward-facing aspect; their main concentrations are on the lower valley slopes.

The relationship between relief, rateable value and race composition appears more clearly in profile (2) across the Berea Ridge. The European section of the University of Natal lies at the peak of the seaward-facing slope, with superb sea and inland views.[1] The highest rateable values are well up on the slope, in predominantly European areas, and decline as we move down towards the Bay, or inland into the Non-European area of Cato Manor. The Berea Ridge cuts off the sea breeze from Cato Manor, which lies on relatively undeveloped land outside the Old Borough. Non-European settlements were established here before there was pressure on Europeans to move into the inland hilly areas.

Profiles (3), (4), (5) and (6) demonstrate the importance of the seaward-facing slopes of the central and northern sections of the Berea Ridge. In profile 5, at Sherwood, we have a European enclave in an inland hilly region, at a height of over 500 feet, where the sea breeze is felt. This is of more recent settlement than the surrounding Non-European areas. Increasing density of development on the seaward-facing slopes has forced Europeans into the inland hilly areas of the city, where the same standards of desirability apply, and to the high hill crests beyond the city boundaries.

The crest of a seaward-facing slope is not necessarily the highest point in rateable values. In profile (4) the continuity

[1] The Non-European section of the University is in the Alluvial Flats of the Old Borough.

of the seaward-facing slope is broken by a valley, with
a municipal park, between the two crests: rateable value is
lower at the second, and higher, crest, and there is incipient
change in racial character. In profile (5), with a similar
formation, rateable values decline in the valley but rise
again towards the second crest, and then fall away in the
Non-European inland areas.

The crest of a seaward-facing slope is generally a boundary
line between the races. Immediately inland from the crest,
race composition begins to change, and in some areas a racial
ambiguity extends to the crests, affecting both the type of
development and the rateable value. Thus, behind the crest
occupied by the University, the division between European
and Non-European is clearly defined by the road pattern.
European homes have moved downwards and occupy
a semi-circular band along the hillside, well-served by tarred
roads, while below them lie the older homes of Indians, for
the most part on unmade streets. The only link between the
two areas is by footpath. At the crest line, a quarter-mile
farther North, however, the areas merge. It is difficult to
state precisely how the observer knows that he is moving
from a European into a mixed, and finally into an Indian,
area. Pavements are not so well made or they are unmade,
roads become narrower and the road pattern is irregular;
there may be distinctive architectural features, or Hindu
religious symbols of bamboo poles with small cloth flags,
while the homes themselves are not so carefully fenced to
stake the owners' property rights against the world. The
movement down the inland slope, like that down the seaward-
facing slope, is a movement towards poverty and cultural
difference.

These cross-sections illustrate in a general way the effect
of climate and topography. Where the Sea Front is developed
it tends to be European and rateable values are relatively
high. The Alluvial Flats form a trough in rateable values of
residential properties and are generally Non-European in

character. Rateable values increase along the seaward-facing slopes, declining again over the crest, while racial composition changes from European to Non-European, save at high altitudes in the inland hilly region.

For purposes of more precise analysis, we have divided the area of Durban into six sociographic zones, so as to take account of these topographical features. The first zone, the Sea Front (Zone I on Figure 13, p. 108), extends along the coast and the bay from north to south. It includes the developed land along the sea front, that is to say, the northern section of the Berea Ridge, the city centre, the Point, the Esplanade, and the Ocean Ridge of the Bluff. Then follow the Alluvial Flats (II). The Central Berea Ridge comprises two zones, areas with high elevation (Central Berea Ridge, Zone IV) and areas with lower elevation (Seaward Transitional, Zone III) between the Alluvial Flats and the upper ridge. The inland hilly areas are also grouped into two zones, a Peripheral Zone (VI) consisting of settlements on the boundaries of the city, which includes most of the Umbilo-Umhlatuzana Interfluve, and an Inland Transitional Zone (V).

A comparison of Figures 11 (p. 97) and 13 (p. 108) shows the relationship between these sociographic zones and the physiographic regions discussed earlier.[1]

[1] There are many departures from the purely geographic divisions. The Ridge extends north and south, but we have separated out the Central Ridge as a distinct feature, since it is regarded in this way by local residents, and since it is an area of early, and dense, settlement. At the same time, we have divided the Central Ridge into two zones, so as to facilitate analysis of the effects of height above sea level. The northern section of the Ridge, the Bluff, the city centre and the Esplanade, are grouped together, though they are distinct geographically. Both Durban North and the Bluff rise directly from the sea, and thus share with residential development on the bay an intimate linkage with the sea. The undeveloped areas on the Sea Front (near the Umgeni River and in the extreme south) are included in census tracts within the Alluvial zone. The Peripheral zone is almost entirely an inland hilly region, but includes most of the Umbilo-Umhlatuzana Interfluve, and the southern portion of the ridge. The purpose of the distinction between the Inland Transitional and the Peripheral zone is to give weight to the factor of distance from the city centre.

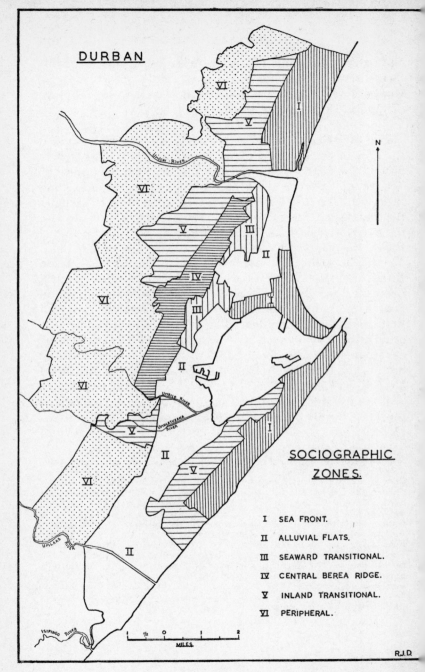

DURBAN

SOCIOGRAPHIC
ZONES.

I SEA FRONT.

II ALLUVIAL FLATS.

III SEAWARD TRANSITIONAL.

IV CENTRAL BEREA RIDGE.

V INLAND TRANSITIONAL.

VI PERIPHERAL.

N

½ 0 1 2
MILES.

R.J.D.

FIGURE 13

Each zone consists of a number of units, which we will refer to as census tracts. These are based on the 262 enumerators' sub-districts used in the 1951 Census of Durban. The Director of Census, owing to heavy commitments, could not provide the basic census data, other than racial composition, in respect of each of these sub-districts, and we were,

TABLE XXIV

RACIAL COMPOSITION OF THE SOCIOGRAPHIC ZONES, DURBAN: 1951 CENSUS

SOCIO-GRAPHIC ZONES	PERCENTAGES					
	Europeans	Coloureds	Indians	Africans	Total	All Non-Europeans
Alluvial Flats	4·69	4·73	55·35	35·23	100·00	95·31
Peripheral .	11·73	2·65	37·49	48·13	100·00	88·27
Inland Transitional	22·08	6·91	55·24	15·77	100·00	77·92
Seaward Transitional	59·45	6·61	15·66	18·28	100·00	40·55
Sea Front .	62·45	0·64	5·44	31·47	100·00	37·55
Central Berea Ridge .	72·63	0·63	1·56	25·18	100·00	27·37
TOTAL .	30·51	3·83	33·98	31·68	100·00	69·49

therefore, obliged to consolidate them. We first grouped together adjacent sub-districts of similar racial composition, and then sub-divided some of the larger groupings so as to take account of differences in rateable value, land use and type of development. The 36 census tracts derived in this way were reviewed by two members of the race-zoning Technical Sub-Committee of the Durban City Council, and submitted to the Director of Census, who agreed to prepare tables of census data for each of these tracts. Unfortunately, the census tracts cover only the city of Durban, and the exclusion of the dormitory towns outside Durban renders our picture of the residential distribution incomplete.[1]

The racial composition of the sociographic zones is shown in Table XXIV (page 109), which gives the percentage which

TABLE XXV

RACIAL COMPOSITION OF THE SOCIOGRAPHIC ZONES (EXCLUDING NON-EUROPEAN DOMESTIC SERVANTS IN PRIVATE HOUSEHOLDS), DURBAN: 1951 CENSUS

SOCIO-GRAPHIC ZONES	PERCENTAGES					
	Europeans	Coloureds	Indians	Africans	Total	All Non-Europeans
Alluvial Flats	4·81	4·81	56·59	33·79	100·00	95·19
Peripheral .	12·48	2·75	39·70	45·07	100·00	87·52
Inland Transitional	23·18	7·16	57·66	12·00	100·00	76·82
Seaward Transitional	65·91	7·18	17·22	9·69	100·00	34·09
Sea Front* .	67·43	0·62	5·83	26·12	100·00	32·57
Central Berea Ridge .	88·59	0·43	1·78	9·20	100·00	11·41
TOTAL .	32·75	4·01	36·28	26·96	100·00	67·25

* If we subtract the barrack population of Africans on the Point, then the respective percentages for the Sea Front zone become 78·27 European, 0·71 Coloured, 6·76 Indian, 14·26 African, and total Non-European 21·73.

each race constitutes of the total population in the zone. The zones are arranged roughly in order of desirability for European residence, in terms of seaward aspect, altitude, and accessibility to the city centre. The percentages in each

[1] In Appendix B we give the numbers of the enumerators' sub-districts included in each census tract, the racial composition of the census tracts, and the numbers of the census tracts in each sociographic zone. The boundaries of the census tracts were determined by the boundaries of the enumerators' sub-districts and do not fall precisely within the physiographic divisions of Durban, outlined above.

column from the first row to the last, therefore, relate the desirability of an area to its racial composition.

Reading down the first column, it is clear that the desirable zones are predominantly European, the percentages ranging

TABLE XXVI

DISTRIBUTION OF EACH RACIAL GROUP IN THE SOCIOGRAPHIC ZONES, DURBAN: 1951 CENSUS

SOCIO-GRAPHIC ZONES	PERCENTAGES					
	Europeans	Coloureds	Indians	Africans	Total	All Non-Europeans
Alluvial Flats	3·25	26·15	34·50	23·56	21·18	29·06
Peripheral .	9·97	17·90	28·62	39·42	25·94	32·95
Inland Transitional	12·83	32·00	28·83	8·83	17·73	19·89
Seaward Transitional	22·65	20·04	5·36	6·71	11·62	6·78
Sea Front .	28·72	2·35	2·25	13·94	14·04	7·58
Central Berea Ridge .	22·58	1·56	0·44	7·54	9·49	3·74
TOTAL .	100·00	100·00	100·00	100·00	100·00	100·00

from 4·69 on the Alluvial Flats to 72·63 on the Central Berea Ridge. Each of the three zones with seaward aspect has a majority of Europeans.

The figures (Table XXIV) mask the residential character of the zones, since they include Non-European domestic servants living in the homes of their European employers, for the most part in backyards. These domestic servants are a large proportion of all domestic servants employed in private households, and we have, therefore, excluded the entire category of private domestic servants in Table XXV.[1]

[1] The census data did not enable us to separate private domestic servants living in Non-European areas but going out to work in European homes, nor could we separate the many domestic servants not working in private households but living on their employers' premises—employees in hotels, boarding-houses, nursing-homes, flats, etc.

The predominantly European character of the desirable areas becomes more marked. The relevant percentages are 65·91 for the Seaward Transitional Zone (as compared with 59·45 when Non-European domestic servants are included),

TABLE XXVII

DISTRIBUTION OF EACH RACIAL GROUP IN THE SOCIOGRAPHIC ZONES (EXCLUDING NON-EUROPEAN DOMESTIC SERVANTS IN PRIVATE HOUSEHOLDS), DURBAN: 1951 CENSUS

SOCIO-GRAPHIC ZONES	PERCENTAGES					
	Europeans	Coloureds	Indians	Africans	Total	All Non-Europeans
Alluvial Flats	3·25	26·57	34·58	27·78	22·16	31·37
Peripheral .	9·97	17·91	28·62	43·73	26·16	34·05
Inland Transitional	12·83	32·36	28·81	8·07	18·13	20·70
Seaward Transitional	22·65	20·13	5·34	4·05	11·25	5·71
Sea Front .	28·72	2·14	2·24	13·52*	13·95	6·75
Central Berea Ridge .	22·58	0·89	0·41	2·85	8·35	1·42
TOTAL .	100·00	100·00	100·00	100·00	100·00	100·00

* If we exclude the barrack population of Africans on the Point, the percentage of the total African population living in the Sea Front areas is reduced to 6·85 per cent.

67·43 compared with 62·45 for the Sea Front zone, and 88·59 on the Berea Ridge as against 72·63.

As is to be expected from the predominantly European character of the more desirable zones, most of the European population lives in these areas. Tables XXVI and XXVII give the distribution of each racial group in the six sociographic zones, the second table excluding domestic servants in private households.

Over half the European population lives on the Central

Berea Ridge and the Sea Front, as compared with 8·17 per cent, or about one-twelfth of Non-Europeans (Table XXVII).[1] Conversely, the main concentrations of Non-European settlement are in the Peripheral zone and the Alluvial Flats, which accommodate almost two-thirds of the Non-European population and less than one-seventh of Europeans. A line drawn mid-way across Table XXVII, that is between the Inland Transitional and the Seaward Transitional zones, divides the predominantly European from the predominantly Non-European areas, the areas which have seaward aspect from those which have none or only a restricted aspect. Thus, 33·55 per cent of the total population lives in the Seaward Transitional, Sea Front and Berea Ridge areas, as compared with 73·95 per cent of the European population. That is to say, over twice as many Europeans (2·20) live in these areas as would be expected if there were an even racial distribution. Conversely, 13·88 per cent of the total Non-European population lives in these areas, or two-fifths (0·41) of what would be expected on the assumption of an even racial distribution.

With some exceptions the general racial character of each zone is relatively constant throughout the census tracts of which it is composed. In the three Central Berea Ridge tracts (11, 12 and 14), Europeans are 89·02 per cent, 89·01 per cent and 87·75 per cent, respectively, of all residents. Almost one quarter (22·58 per cent) of the total European population lives in these tracts, as compared with 1·42 per cent of Non-Europeans (0·89 per cent Coloureds, 0·41 per cent Indians and 2·85 per cent Africans).

So, too, in the Sea Front zone, four of the six census tracts

[1] The figures given above and throughout the remainder of this chapter (excluding the final section dealing with the Old Borough and Added areas), are exclusive of Non-European private domestic servants, but include all other Non-European employees living on premises provided by their employers. They therefore overstate the extent of Non-European residence in the desirable areas. We can assume, in general, that Africans shown as living on the Central Berea Ridge and in other desirable areas are workers living in accommodation provided by their employers.

H

have a large proportion of Europeans (72·93 per cent in tract 32 on the Ocean Ridge of the Bluff; 81·08 per cent in the Central City, tract 17; 82·69 per cent on the Esplanade, tract 19; and 92·48 per cent in Durban North, tract 3). In tract 36, which includes military, defence and dock installations on the Point, a section of the Bluff and Salisbury Island, the large numbers of Africans are mainly dock-workers housed in barracks, while the residential areas are European. Only the racial composition of tract 5, the suburbs of Prospect Hall and Riverside immediately north of the Umgeni River mouth, and a small section of the Ocean Ridge on the Bluff, depart from the general principle of the occupation of the Sea Front zone by Europeans.[1] Tract 5 is an area of Indian residential settlement, with Indians constituting 89·30 per cent of the residents. In the Sea Front Zone as a whole there are 28·72 per cent of Europeans as compared with 6·75 per cent of Non-Europeans (2·14 per cent of Coloureds, 2·24 per cent of Indians and 13·52 per cent of Africans, the latter being housed mainly in barracks and compounds).

Moving to the two main Non-European zones, we find Non-European dominance maintained in each of the seven census tracts in the Alluvial Zone. The percentage of Non-Europeans varies from 87·50 to 99·78.[2] Only 3·25 per cent

---

[1] The elevation in tract 5 is not marked. Most of the area lies under 100 feet above sea level, and all of it under 200 feet. The area overlooks a swamp, but has become more attractive with the development of highways.

Both tracts 7 and 33, classified as Alluvial, have frontage to the sea. In neither area has the sea front been developed.

[2]

Census Tract No.	% Non-European
7	98·69
16	87·50
18	92·46
28	99·78
29	99·76
30	97·53
33	90·69

The percentages are of nearly the same dimensions when Non-European private domestic servants are included.

of Europeans lives in this zone, as compared with 31·37 per cent of Non-Europeans; that is, in absolute figures, only one European to every twenty Non-Europeans. Sections of these Alluvial Flats were malarial swamps as late as 1934, when the city had its last serious outbreak of malaria.[1] Land in this residentially undesirable belt was either allotted for Non-European barracks, compounds and locations, or occupied by Non-Europeans on their own initiative.

The census tracts in the Peripheral Zone are more varied in character, since they include the southern section of the ridge, and the Umbilo-Umhlatuzana Interfluve. Five of the eight tracts have a substantial Non-European majority, the percentage ranging from 87·79 per cent to 99·95 per cent,[2] while the southern section of the ridge (tract 34) and the higher slopes of the interfluve (tract 25) are European in character (81·70 per cent and 79·90 per cent respectively). The remaining tract, 26 on the lower slopes of the interfluve, is intermediate in racial composition, with a Non-European majority, but a substantial proportion of Europeans (39·68 per cent). All told, the percentage of Non-Europeans living in the Peripheral Zone is almost four times as high as that of Europeans (34·05 per cent as compared with 9·97 per cent).

The Inland Transitional tracts are of the same varied character as those in the Peripheral Zone. The predominantly Non-European character of the zone as a whole is maintained in five of its seven census tracts, with percentages varying

---

[1] All told, 1,154 cases were notified, while the death roll amounted to 248. This outbreak speeded up the work of reclamation and the drainage of swamps, which was well advanced by 1936, and has now solved the problem of malarial control.

[2]

Census Tract No.	% Non-European
1	87·79
6	97·65
23	95·30
24	99·95
35	99·47

from 75·57 per cent to 98·62 per cent.[1] Two of the census tracts (tract 2, which adjoins the highly desirable Durban North Ridge, and tract 31, which includes the Bay Ridge on the Bluff) have a European majority, the relevant percentages being 79·19 and 52·56 respectively. The zone accommodates 20·70 per cent of Non-Europeans and 12·83 per cent of Europeans.

The most marked racial intermingling occurs in the tracts of the Seaward Transitional zone. Its extent is, however, overstated by the figures for racial composition, since there is segregation within the census tracts. Indeed, the term 'interdigitation' is sometimes used to describe the interweaving in the marginal sections between the European and Non-European settlements.

The zone is predominantly European: 22·65 per cent of Europeans as compared with 5·71 per cent of Non-Europeans live here. Tract 13, with a Non-European percentage of 67·01, deviates from the general pattern of European dominance. It is one of the oldest areas of residential settlement in Durban, and 'transitional' in the sense in which the term was used by the Chicago school of urban sociologists. Commerce and small industrial establishments, that is to say, have invaded the area, with deterioration in its quality for residential purposes and a measure of blight, though not nearly so extensive as would be expected from the American studies.

The higher slopes (tracts 10 and 15) are markedly European, with percentages of 87·25 and 88·19, and tract 8, on the fringe of the Berea, is still largely European (67·10 per cent). Tract 9, however, which lies well up on the Central Berea Ridge, is less European in character (58·06

	Census Tract No.	% Non-European
[1]	4	90·55
	20	81·09
	21	96·82
	22	98·62
	27	75·57

per cent European) and has a substantial proportion of Indian residents (26·70 per cent as compared with 14·69 per cent in tract 8). It constitutes an exception to the general rule of a decline in the proportion of Non-Europeans with increasing height above sea level. There is a 'natural' zone of Indian settlement based on the Alluvial Flats of the Old Borough (tract 7, with its barracks population, and tract 18), and on the transitional tract 13, and extending upwards into the Berea in tract 9. In these four tracts is concentrated 87·33 per cent of the total Indian population of the Old Borough.

This distinction between the Old Borough and the Added Areas is of considerable ecological significance, taking account, as it does, of the growth of the city. The Old Borough comprises most of the land between the Umgeni and Umbilo Rivers, extending west to the top of the Central Berea Ridge.[1] The Indian population settled mainly in the areas outside the Borough boundaries, with the result that, on the incorporation of these areas in 1932, the racial composition of the city was transformed. Europeans constituted 47·20 per cent of the Old Borough population in 1932, but only 36·21 per cent of the total population of the city in 1933, while the Indian percentage rose from 14·68 per cent to 31·71 per cent.[2]

The difference in racial composition between the Old Borough and the Added Areas persists to the present day. Over two-thirds of the European population lives in the Old Borough, while, in contrast, almost four-fifths of the Indian population and nearly two-thirds of the Coloured population live in the less developed Added Areas.

---

[1] Census tracts 7–19 inclusive, and 36, which extends beyond the Old Borough boundaries. Tract 20 straddles the boundaries, but falls largely outside the Old Borough.

[2]

YEAR		RACE				
		Europeans	Coloureds	Indians	Africans	Total
1932	. .	59,480	4,290	18,500	43,750	126,020
1933	. .	79,600	4,910	69,710	64,610	219,830

TABLE XXVIII

PERCENTAGE DISTRIBUTION OF RACES IN THE OLD BOROUGH AND THE ADDED AREAS, DURBAN: 1951 CENSUS

Area	Europeans %	Coloureds %	Indians %	Africans %	Total Population
Old Borough .	68·66	36·81	21·21	45·05	43·84
Added Areas .	31·34	63·19	78·79	54·95	56·16

Note.—The tracts for which we have Census data do not correspond exactly with the areas of the Old Borough. The differences are, however, very small. This table includes Non-European domestic servants in private households. The percentages, excluding these domestic servants, are of roughly the same order: Coloureds, 36·35 per cent in the Old Borough, Indians, 21·18 per cent, and Africans, 43·08 per cent.

Africans are divided between the old and new sections of the city in roughly the same proportion as the total population, indicating a general dependence on African labour. However, the African population of the Old Borough consists mostly of single men or married men, living away

TABLE XXIX

SEX RATIOS OF RACES IN THE OLD BOROUGH AND THE ADDED AREAS, DURBAN: 1951 CENSUS

Area	Europeans %	Coloureds %	Indians %	Africans %	Total Population
Old Borough .	0·93	0·81	1·06	4·40	1·47
Added Areas .	0·98	0·92	1·03	1·38	1·11
Greater Durban	0·95	0·88	1·04	2·18	1·26

Note.—Table includes Non-European domestic servants in private households.

from their families, in compounds or as domestic servants. The African masculinity rate of 440 males for every 100 females in the Old Borough contrasts with a rate of 138 in the Added Areas.

The residential distribution of African *families* is similar to that of Indian and Coloured families—mainly in the Added Areas of Durban.

CHAPTER V

RESIDENTIAL ECOLOGY OF THE RACES (CONTINUED): INCOME, RELIGION AND LANGUAGE

In this chapter our figures are inclusive of Non-European domestic servants, since we are discussing the variations within each racial group.

THE distribution of income, religious and language groups within each race shows a pattern related to the climate and topography of the city. This pattern is clearly defined in the case of the Europeans, among whom competition for the more desirable areas is unrestricted. Income is the most significant factor, and in Figure 14 we relate the *per capita* income of Europeans to general standards of residential desirability—elevation above sea level, seaward aspect, and sea frontage.[1]

The general pattern of income conforms roughly to the physical contours of the city (compare Figure 14 with Figure 10, p. 96). The highest *per capita* income (over £500 per annum) is to be found in tract 11, towards the crest of the Central Berea Ridge.[2] High incomes extend along the

---

[1] This map is only approximate and designed to give a general picture. We have the *per capita* income for each of the census tracts, giving us fixed points of reference, between which we have interpolated estimates of *per capita* income. We have also indicated areas of higher class housing within a tract, as, for example, on the Northern Berea Ridge, the Ocean Ridge of the Bluff, and the Umgeni-Umbilo watershed in the Inland Hilly region. The map thus goes beyond the actual income data, and presents more gradual and regular gradients than the data warrant. In tracts 28, 29, 30, 33, all on the Alluvial Flats in the south, income varies from £124·74 to £156·34. Average income for the 4 tracts is below £150, and we have treated the tracts as one unit.

[2] Appendix C (p. 241) gives the mean and *per capita* incomes, by race, in each of the census tracts.

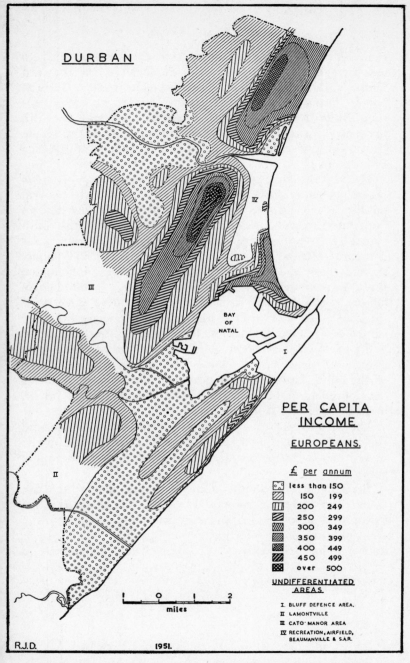

DURBAN

PER CAPITA
INCOME

EUROPEANS.

£ per annum

- less than 150
- 150 199
- 200 249
- 250 299
- 300 349
- 350 399
- 400 449
- 450 499
- over 500

UNDIFFERENTIATED
AREAS

I. BLUFF DEFENCE AREA.
II LAMONTVILLE
III CATO MANOR AREA
IV RECREATION, AIRFIELD,
BEAUMANVILLE & S.A.R.

BAY
OF
NATAL

miles

R.J.D.   1951.

FIGURE 14: ISOMETRIC MAP—EUROPEAN *PER CAPITA* INCOME

remaining Central Berea Ridge tracts, declining as the ridge falls away to the Umlaas River in the south, to the Seaward Transitional zone and the Alluvial Flats in the east, and the Inland Transitional zone in the west. So, too, the concentration of high *per capita* income (between £350 and £400) in the coastal areas of Durban North (tract 3) and the Esplanade (tract 19) demonstrates the selective influence of the Sea Front zone.

The Ocean Ridge on the Bluff, with an average *per capita* income of under £250 per annum, deviates from the general pattern.[1] The Bluff is in the southern sector of the city, in the Added Areas south of the Umbilo River, and the south generally is relatively poor. There are no high income areas comparable with Durban North or the Central Berea Ridge, though there is a narrow line of high-cost housing on the Bluff, immediately overlooking the beach. A number of factors probably account for this comparative poverty of the south. It is orientated topographically away from the centre of the city, and access lies through industrial zones, and poor dwellings, often shacks, of the Indian population living on the Alluvial Flats. The seaward-facing slopes of the Bluff are steep and provide little land suitable for development, while the Bluff itself cuts off most of the inland areas in the south from the sea breezes.

The selective character of the Central Berea Ridge and the Sea Front is shown in Table XXX, which relates the mean and *per capita* incomes of Europeans to sociographic zone.

Reading down columns 2 and 3, mean income increases from £407·59 in the Alluvial Flats to £583·22 on the Sea Front and £705·36 on the Central Berea Ridge, while *per capita* income increases from £210·17 to £334·71 and £368·26 respectively. Income levels in residential

---

[1] Tract 5 also deviates from the pattern. It has moderate elevation and seaward aspect (see footnote [1], p. 114), but the *per capita* income of Europeans living there is under £200. However, this is an Indian area with only 43 Europeans.

areas are related to elevation, seaward aspect, and sea frontage.[1]

In column 1 of Table XXX, we have included the ratio of Europeans to Indians, so as to show the relationship

TABLE XXX

MEAN AND *PER CAPITA* INCOME OF EUROPEANS, BY SOCIOGRAPHIC ZONES, AND BY RATIO OF EUROPEANS TO INDIANS, DURBAN: 1951 CENSUS

SOCIOGRAPHIC ZONES	(1) RATIO *Europeans : Indians*	(2) MEAN INCOME £ per annum	(3) *Per Capita* INCOME £ per annum
Alluvial Flats . .	0·08	407·59	210·17
Peripheral . .	0·31	484·27	204·26
Inland Transitional .	0·40	479·25	205·18
Seaward Transitional	3·80	430·78	219·94
Sea Front . .	11·47	583·22	334·71
Central Berea Ridge	46·47	705·36	368·26
TOTAL . .	0·90	552·06	282·74

[1] The relationship between topographical features and income is most clear in the Alluvial Flats, the Sea Front and the Central Berea Ridge. For the rest, the broad grouping of census tracts in the zones obscures the relationship. In the Seaward Transitional zone mean income varies with elevation, from £378 and £396 on the lower slopes (tracts 8 and 13) to £429, £442 and £506 on the upper slopes (15, 9, 10): *per capita* incomes show a similar range, from £178 to £282. Again, in the Inland Transitional and Peripheral zones, in tract 4 (which includes land immediately adjoining the northern ridge), tract 20 (nearest the Central Berea ridge), tract 23 (with an elevated European enclave), and tract 34 (on the southern ridge), mean incomes are appreciably higher than in any of the Alluvial tracts. *Per capita* incomes are also higher, save in relation to Alluvial tract 7, which has a small European population towards the sea front.

The distinction between the Old Borough and the Added Areas is important: three of the Alluvial tracts fall within the Old Borough, and these have lower dependency rates and higher *per capita* incomes than the remaining four Alluvial tracts in the southern districts of the Added Areas. It is these Old Borough tracts which raise the overall *per capita* income of European residents on the Alluvial Flats.

between European mean and *per capita* income in an area and the proportion of Indians residing there. The highest ratios of Europeans to Indians are in the high-income zones of the Sea Front and the Central Berea Ridge. In other words, the proportion of Indians may be used as an index of the most desirable European areas and of the highest economic levels among the European residents.[1]

The distribution of income groups among the Indian population follows an entirely different pattern from that of Europeans. The main distinction is between the Old Borough and the Added Areas, with *per capita* incomes of £62·23 and £34·04 respectively. It was possible in the past, as it is today, for Indians to establish themselves at lower cost outside the Old Borough, and this no doubt explains the greater impoverishment of Indian residents in the Added Areas. In none of the census tracts in these Added Areas does the *per capita* income of Indians rise above £50 per annum (Figure 15, p. 127).

The *per capita* income of Europeans is also lower in the Added Areas (£234·32 as compared with £304·75 in the Old Borough), but the mean income is roughly the same. The difference in *per capita* income is due to the higher dependency rates of the European population in the Added Areas.[2] In the case of the Indian population, however, the main factor in the lower *per capita* income of the Added Areas is lower earning capacity (a mean income of £160·32 as against £255·83 in the Old Borough).

Within the Old Borough itself the distribution of Indian

[1] Tract 9 in the Seaward Transitional zone, as we have seen, is a marked exception to the general rule of a declining Indian population with increasing height above sea level, combined with seaward aspect. So, too, tract 5, an area of Indian settlement, is the main exception to the general occupation of the Sea Front by Europeans.

[2] The population of the Added Areas is generally younger in age structure —50 per cent is under 21, as compared with 31 per cent in the Old Borough. The difference is slight for Coloureds and Indians, and most marked for Africans. Among Europeans, lower median age, as well as lower rates for the widowed and divorced, in the Added Areas indicate the attraction of the more open suburbs of Durban for young families with growing children.

income also does not conform to the European pattern. Two of the tracts on the Central Berea Ridge, with a small population of Indians, have high incomes; the third, which includes poor Indian settlements along the slopes towards the Umbilo River, has among the lowest. In the Sea Front tracts, incomes are also low, except for the two central tracts, which, however, house few Indians. The highest *per capita* incomes are found in the Seaward Transitional zone, tracts 10 and 15, but these, again, have few Indian residents (123 and 53 respectively).[1] The main concentration of groups, with fairly high incomes and represented by large numbers of residents, is in the alluvial tract 18, adjoining the city centre, and in the transitional tract 13, between the city centre and the lower slopes of the Central Berea Ridge.[2] These two tracts, extending into the adjoining lower slopes of the central ridge (tracts 8 and 9), form the basis of a distinctive area of Indian settlement not only in terms of racial composition (page 117), but also in terms of relatively high income.

Table XXXI shows the distribution of mean and *per capita* incomes of the Indian population in the six sociographic zones.

The lowest incomes are in the areas farthest from the city centre, the Peripheral and Inland Transitional zones. Then follow the Sea Front and the Alluvial Flats, but this is a broad grouping which obscures the distinction between the tracts with relatively high income in the Old Borough, and the tracts with low income in the Added Areas. The highest incomes are found in the two Old Borough zones, the Seaward Transitional with mean income of £330·23 and *per capita* income of £86·09, and the Central Berea Ridge with

---

[1] This settlement was part of the movement of more well-to-do Indians into the desirable European areas, a process immediately arrested by legislative action.

[2] *Per capita* income is £74·86 for tract 13 and £70·80 for tract 18: mean income is £280·31 and £293·29. Of the 756 Indians earning more than £600 per annum, almost half (347) live in these two tracts, though their population is about one-eighth of the total.

mean income £279·02 and *per capita* income £87·30. Clearly, proximity to the commercial centre is the most important factor in the residential distribution of the higher income groups in the Indian population, though elevation above sea level and seaward aspect also operate as standards of desirability. Partly, however, because of the poverty of

TABLE XXXI

MEAN AND *PER CAPITA* INCOME OF INDIANS, BY SOCIOGRAPHIC ZONES, DURBAN: 1951 CENSUS

SOCIOGRAPHIC ZONES	MEAN INCOME £ per annum	*Per Capita* INCOME £ per annum
Alluvial Flats . . .	185·58	41·39
Peripheral	156·79	32·88
Inland Transitional . . .	168·74	35·81
Seaward Transitional . .	330·23	86·09
Sea Front	187·71	44·97
Central Berea Ridge . .	279.02	87·30
TOTAL . .	182·85	40·02

Indians relative to Europeans, and partly because of restrictions on the free play of the property market, the effective choice for the more wealthy Indians has been between homes in the Added Areas, and homes on the lower slopes of the Central Berea Ridge or in the Alluvial Flats of the Old Borough. They preferred the more centrally situated residential districts.

For the African population, the relevant income data are not available, while among the Coloured population the distribution of incomes does not show a distinctive pattern. The range of variation is narrow, and Coloureds are scattered in relatively small numbers throughout the census tracts, apart from five tracts which house half their

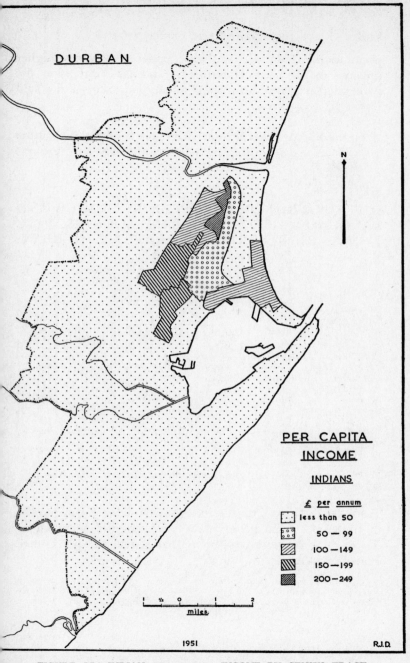

DURBAN

N

PER CAPITA
INCOME

INDIANS

£ per annum
less than 50
50 — 99
100 — 149
150 — 199
200 — 249

1 ½ 0 1 2
miles.

1951   R.J.D.

FIGURE 15: INDIAN *PER CAPITA* INCOME BY CENSUS TRACT

population. There is a slight tendency towards higher incomes in the areas favoured by Indians—that is, in the Alluvial tracts and Seaward Transitional zone of the Old Borough.

The ecological distribution of income is at the same time an ecological distribution of religious and language groups.

TABLE XXXII

DISTRIBUTION OF EUROPEAN RELIGIOUS AND LANGUAGE GROUPS IN THE SOCIOGRAPHIC ZONES, REPRESENTED BY RATIOS,* DURBAN: 1951 CENSUS

SOCIOGRAPHIC ZONES	RELIGIOUS GROUPS				LANGUAGE GROUPS	
	Jewish	Christian			English	Afrikaans
		Afrikaans Protestant	Roman Catholic	Other Christian		
Alluvial Flats .	0·35	2·23	1·08	0·80	0·76	2·45
Peripheral .	0·23	1·44	0·97	0·96	0·92	1·52
Inland Transi-tional . . .	0·34	1·46	0·96	0·96	0·91	1·58
Seaward Transi-tional . . .	0·51	1·17	1·24	0·95	0·97	1·17
Sea Front .	1·51	0·79	0·86	1·03	1·04	0·72
Central Berea Ridge . . .	1·66	0·47	0·96	1·08	1·10	0·42

* Percentage of European Language or Religious Group in Zone: Percentage of Europeans in Zone.

Table XXXII presents the relevant data for Europeans in the form of a ratio between the percentage of a particular language or religious group in a zone, and the percentage of all Europeans in that zone.[1]

[1] A ratio of 1 indicates that the distribution of the language or religious group is the same as that of the European population as a whole: a ratio above 1 indicates concentration, and less than one, under-representation.

The Jewish population, with highest income, is concentrated in the more desirable areas (ratios of 1·66 and 1·51 for the Central Berea Ridge and Sea Front zones respectively), while under-representation is most marked in the peripheral area. The Jewish group, largely professional, trading and industrial, is essentially a city population: 85·03 per cent live in the Old Borough.

The distribution of the members of the Afrikaans Protestant Churches is the reverse of the Jewish population. They have low mean and *per capita* incomes and are concentrated in the Alluvial Flats (a ratio of 2·23), in the inland areas (1·44 and 1·46), and to a lesser extent in the Seaward Transitional zone (1·17), while they are under-represented on the Sea Front and the Central Berea Ridge (0·79 and 0·47 respectively). So, too, the Roman Catholic population, with the lowest *per capita* income, is concentrated, though not heavily, in the Seaward Transitional and Alluvial zones, and is under-represented on the Sea Front. For the rest, the distribution of Roman Catholics is much the same as that of the European population as a whole.

The distribution of language groups is related to that of religious groups. In general, the more desirable the area, the higher the concentration of English-speaking residents, and the greater the under-representation of the Afrikaans-speaking. From the figures in Table XXXII, we may derive the suggestion that some Afrikaans-speaking residents in the poorer areas are not members of the Afrikaans Protestant Churches, and conversely that, in the richer areas, some members of the Afrikaans Protestant Churches do not use Afrikaans as their home language. There may be a tendency among the more well-to-do Afrikaners in Durban to shed Afrikaans as the home language.

Occupation and status of employment are associated with income, and show a distribution related to the desirability of the area of living. Thus, the major concentration of European men in the census category of professional,

I

technical and related workers, and of employers, is on the Central Berea Ridge (ratios of 1·52 and 1·55 respectively),[1] the lowest on the Alluvial Flats (0·62 and 0·35). Skilled metal workers, though fairly evenly distributed, are least represented on the Central Berea Ridge (a ratio of 0·75) and most concentrated in the Peripheral and Seaward Transitional zones (both 1·16). Again, the largest ratio for unemployed men is on the Alluvial Flats (3·10), the smallest on the Ridge (0·45). Other demographic characteristics of the European population also cluster in a pattern often found in western industrial society.[2]

Among the Indian population, the higher earning capacity of Muslims and Christians, of the Gujarati and the English-speaking, is reflected in their distribution (Table XXXIII, p. 132). Muslims and Christians are heavily concentrated in the high-income Seaward Transitional zone (ratios of 2·09 and 2·18), while the Hindus are under-represented (0·65). So, too, among the language groups, between three and four times as many English- and Gujarati-speaking Indians are found in the Seaward Transitional zone as would be expected on an even distribution of language groups; and, conversely,

[1] The northern section of the ridge, in tract 3, has even higher concentrations (1·63 and 1·89).
[2] The high income zones of the Central Berea Ridge and the Sea Front have a concentration of widowed persons (ratios of 1·14 and 1·17): the population is mature (with 69·05 per cent, and 74·55 per cent over 21) and women are in the majority (the masculinity rates being 85·7 and 94·0). The Sea Front zone has, in fact, the highest proportion of mature persons, and of the widowed and the divorced (1·58 as compared with 0·75 for the Berea Ridge). Clearly Durban, as a seaside resort, attracts these persons to its beaches from other parts of the Union. In the two inland, more suburban, zones are found the lowest ratios for the widowed* and divorced* (less than 0·70 and 0·50 respectively), the youngest age structure (over 41 per cent under 21), and an equal proportion of men and women, while the Alluvial Flats have the highest masculinity rate (128·8) and a high ratio for divorced persons (1·45). Divorced persons are concentrated at the extremes, in areas of high and low income. The Seaward Transitional zone, in general, is close to the European norm for the city as a whole, in respect of masculinity rate, and proportions of the widowed and divorced.

*Ratios were calculated as follows:
Percentage of Widowed (or Divorced) Europeans in Zone: Percentage of Europeans (over 21 years of age) in Zone.

the Tamil- and Telugu- and particularly the Hindi-speaking are in relatively small numbers (ratios of 0·78, 0·50, and 0·28 respectively). The population in tract 18, a favoured area in the Alluvial Zone of the Old Borough, has much the same characteristics, the concentration of Muslims, English- and Gujarati-speaking, and the sparse settlement by Hindi-speaking; Christian Indians are, however, less represented.

In general, the presence of higher proportions of Gujarati- or English-speaking, of Muslims or Christians, may be taken as an index of higher-income areas, and the presence of higher proportions of Hindi-speaking as an index of low-income areas. Thus, the ratio of Hindi-speaking in the poorest area, the Peripheral zone, is 1·61, that of the Gujarati-speaking is 0·15: conversely, in the Seaward Transitional zone, the richest Indian areas, the corresponding ratios are 0·28 for the Hindi-speaking, and 3·69 for the Gujarati-speaking. Similar differences are found between Christians, Muslims and English-speaking on the one hand, and the Hindus and Hindi-speaking on the other. The Central Berea Ridge appears to be anomalous, with some concentration of Hindi-speaking (1·23), though less than the English-speaking (1·32) or the Gujarati-speaking (3·38). However, the Gujarati- and English-speaking are concentrated in the high-income tracts (11 and 12), and the Hindi-speaking in tract 14, which includes less desirable, low-lying land.

In terms of occupation, there is a relative concentration of professional, technical and related workers in the Seaward Transitional zone (ratio 2·09) and on the Central Berea Ridge (3·10). Employers are concentrated in the same areas (ratios of 2·19 and 2·05 respectively). On the Alluvial Flats only tract 18 in the Old Borough shows similar concentrations, the ratio for professional and related workers being 1·35, and for employers 3·03. There are no other high concentrations, apart from market gardeners in the Peripheral zone and to some extent on the Sea Front.

The distribution of occupations, of language and religious

TABLE XXXIII

DISTRIBUTION OF INDIAN RELIGIOUS AND LANGUAGE GROUPS IN THE SOCIOGRAPHIC ZONES, REPRESENTED BY RATIOS,* DURBAN: 1951 CENSUS

SOCIOGRAPHIC ZONES	RELIGIOUS GROUPS			LANGUAGE GROUPS					
	Hindu	Islamic	Christian	English	Tamil	Hindi	Telugu	Guja-rati	Urdu
Alluvial Flats .	0·98	1·05	1·08	0·87	1·16	0·65	0·98	1·84	0·83
Peripheral . .	1·11	0·66	0·66	0·57	0·84	1·61	1·05	0·15	0·80
Inland Transitional	0·98	1·09	1·05	1·14	1·02	0·94	1·05	0·32	1·42
Seaward Transitional	0·65	2·09	2·18	3·63	0·78	0·28	0·50	3·69	1·17
Sea Front . .	1·12	0·71	0·64	0·46	0·82	1·31	1·39	0·75	0·62
Central Berea Ridge .	0·84	1·51	1·00	1·32	0·84	1·23	0·29	3·38	0·16

* Percentage of Indian Language or Religious Group in Zone: Percentage of Indians in Zone.

groups, partly explains the concentration of higher income in the Old Borough. Over 82 per cent of the Gujarati-speaking, as compared with 21·21 per cent of the entire Indian population, and 5·69 per cent of the Hindi-speaking population,[1] lives in the Old Borough. The percentages of English-speaking Indians in the Old Borough (37·83), of Muslims (36·43), of Christians (32·45), and of employers (43·52) are all higher than the expected distribution. There is a tendency for the trading-classes and the more westernized Indians to live near the centre of the city.[2]

Among the Coloureds, religious, language, and occupational groups do not show a distinctive pattern of distribution. In most of the census tracts, only small numbers are involved, and for this reason the Coloureds on the Central Berea Ridge and the Sea Front, many of them domestic servants, may be disregarded. There is a slight tendency towards concentration of members of Protestant denominations on the periphery, of minor Christian sects in the two transitional zones, and of Coloured Muslims in the tracts favoured by Indian Muslims, reflecting, no doubt, the bond of religious and other interests. Afrikaans-speaking Coloureds, like Afrikaans-speaking Europeans, are heavily represented in the Peripheral zone and the Alluvial Flats.

Among the largely Zulu-speaking African population of Durban, only the Southern Sotho show a marked departure from the expected distribution by a concentration in the Peripheral zone. The distribution of religious groups, however, is distinctively patterned.

[1] The concentration of the Hindi-speaking in the Added Areas (94·31 per cent) is not explained entirely by their poverty. The equally impoverished Tamil and Telugu are less concentrated in these areas (79·73 per cent and 82·75 per cent), and show a greater tendency than the Hindi to cluster round the Bay.

[2] In contrast to the European population, there is no distinctive ecological pattern in the distribution of the widowed and the divorced, and of masculinity rates and of age structure, among the Indian and Coloured populations. The Added Areas, as we have already noted, are slightly younger in age structure.

The main concentration of the category classified as 'Quasi-religious, no religion, unspecified' is in the Alluvial Flats (1·81) and the Sea Front (1·82). These are the zones with high African masculinity rates (711·75 and 606·70), zones with barracks and compounds for migrant workers, still close to the traditional ancestor-worship.[1] The minor

TABLE XXXIV

DISTRIBUTION OF AFRICAN RELIGIOUS GROUPS IN THE SOCIOGRAPHIC ZONES, REPRESENTED BY RATIOS,* DURBAN: 1951 CENSUS

SOCIOGRAPHIC ZONES	RELIGIOUS GROUPS			
	Roman Catholic	Protestant	Minor Sects	Quasi-Religious, No Religion, Unspecified
Alluvial Flats . .	0·85	0·88	1·25	1·81
Peripheral . .	1·11	1·18	0·74	0·36
Inland Transitional .	0·91	0·88	0·99	0·73
Seaward Transitional .	1·01	0·97	0·97	0·90
Sea Front . . .	0·99	0·78	1·23	1·82
Central Berea Ridge .	0·98	1·01	1·20	0·70

* Percentage of African Religious Group in Zone: Percentage of Africans in Zone.

Christian sects, including the African Separatist Churches and religious groups marginal between traditional Bantu worship and Christianity, are also concentrated, though to a small extent, in the same zones (1·25 and 1·23).[2] The Peripheral zone, on the other hand, has the highest ratio

[1] Marriage by lobola provides a further index of adherence to tradition. The highest concentrations of lobola marriages are in the Alluvial Flats (1·45) and the Sea Front (1·35).

[2] The Central Berea Ridge has a similar concentration of minor sects (1·20). The African residents are almost entirely domestic servants, generally drawn from the less urbanized sections of the population.

for the major Christian denominations (1·11 Roman
Catholic and 1·18 Protestant) and the lowest for the quasi-
religious (0·36) and for the minor Christian sects (0·74).
It is an area of family living,[1] with the lowest masculinity
rate (118·71), and the youngest age structure (40·17 per cent
under 21 as compared with 14·33 per cent on the Alluvial
Flats and 17·79 per cent in the Sea Front zone).

These features of the Peripheral zone are characteristic
also of the Added Areas as a whole. The latter are areas of
African family living[2] and of affiliation with the Christian
churches: 62·21 per cent of Roman Catholics and 62·47 per
cent of Protestants live in the Added Areas, while those who
have not specified their religious affiliation, or are classified
as having no religion, are to be found largely in the Old
Borough (73·21 per cent). In terms of occupation, most of
the small professional group, mainly teachers, and virtually
all of the small force of office workers, are housed in the
Added Areas. In contrast to the Indian population, there
is thus a tendency for the more westernized Africans to live
in the Added Areas and on the periphery of the city. It is
here that the new urban African society is emerging.

Our main findings, in regard to the racial ecology of
Durban can now be summarized with the assistance of the
distributions shown in Figures 16–19. The darker the shading
in these distributions, the greater is the concentration of
a particular racial group.[3] Thus, in Figure 16 (p. 137),
dealing with the residential distribution of the European

---

[1] There is also family disorganization in the Peripheral zone, as measured
by the high ratio (1·71) of persons not married, but living together. (These
would generally be living outside the municipal locations.) The corresponding
ratios for the Alluvial Flats and the Sea Front are 0·26 and 0·37.

[2] See page 119.

[3] We have not adjusted the census tables so as to exclude Non-European
domestic servants working in private households, and present the distribution
precisely as given by the Director of Census. The picture of Coloured and
Indian residence is relatively unaffected; that of the African population is
substantially different. In the case of Europeans, most of the heavily shaded
tracts (60–79 per cent) would be one shade darker (over 80 per cent).

population, the peripheral areas are all lightly shaded, apart from the southern extension of the Berea Ridge and the Interfluve. Heavy concentrations lie on the Central Berea Ridge and along the Sea Front. Moving along the coast line from north to south, we have an area of European dominance, followed by a small square of Indian settlement immediately north of the Umgeni River mouth, and a long undeveloped strip, south of the river. Then come the Esplanade and the city centre along the Bay, essentially European in character, the dock and defence installations on the Point, Salisbury Island and the Bluff, the predominantly European Ocean Ridge of the Bluff, and finally the undeveloped southern beach front. Roughly four of every five Europeans live in relatively desirable land—the ridge including the Seaward Transitional zone, high inland enclaves and the Sea Front.

The distribution of Europeans varies with income, the concentration of high-income groups, like that of the European population as a whole, being related to the desirability of the residential area. In general, the southern areas have proved less attractive than the northern and central districts, both as European settlements and for higher-income groups. Since income is associated with occupation, religious affiliation and language, these characteristics also have a well-defined ecological distribution. Marital status, age structure and sex composition vary with the location of the residential areas, and their economic character.

The map of the distribution of Coloureds (Figure 17, p. 139) is all light in shade, since the Coloureds are a small community. Comparing the distribution of Coloureds with that of Europeans, we see immediately that there are very few Coloureds in the areas of European dominance. Either the Coloureds cannot afford to establish themselves in the more desirable areas of the city, or many of the Coloureds who live there pass as Europeans. No doubt both factors operate.

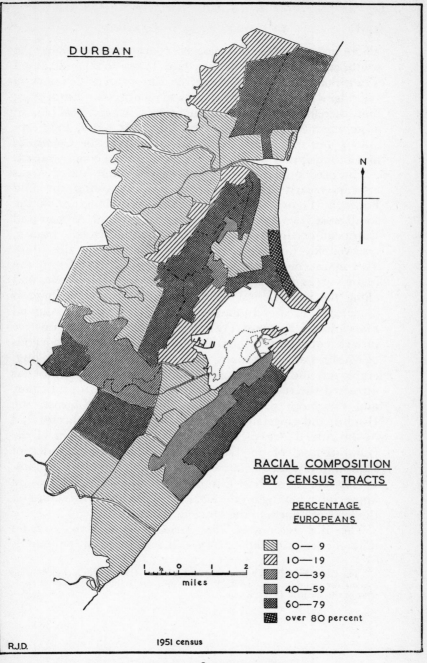

DURBAN

N

RACIAL COMPOSITION
BY CENSUS TRACTS

PERCENTAGE
EUROPEANS

	0— 9
	10—19
	20—39
	40—59
	60—79
	over 80 percent

1 ½ 0 1 2
miles

R.J.D.

1951 census

FIGURE 16: EUROPEANS

There are two areas of Coloured concentration, one in the south, and the other in the Seaward Transitional and Inland Transitional zones,[1] encircling the European settlements on the ridge. Perhaps Coloureds seek to identify with Europeans, and therefore to establish themselves, where possible, in adjoining neighbourhoods. On the other hand, these are among the more desirable residential areas for Coloureds and Indians; they are, in fact, areas of Indian concentration.

The predominantly Indian character of the Added Areas appears clearly from the heavy shading round the Old Borough (Figure 18, p. 140). The exceptions are in the south-west (two tracts, 35 and 34, reserved for African and European occupation respectively), Durban North (tract 3, reserved for Europeans) and to a lesser extent the Bluff. The main concentrations of Indian settlement lie in the inland areas to the north-west, west, and south-east, and along the river banks. Within the Old Borough there is a 'natural' area of Indian settlement based on the Alluvial Flats and the Seaward Transitional zone. This is distinctive in terms of relatively high income, and of high proportions of Muslims and Christians, Gujarati- and English-speaking, employers and professionals. Proximity to the city centre has attracted the traders and professional classes in particular, and the more westernized in general. In contrast, the Hindus, and especially the Hindi-speaking, are concentrated in the Added Areas. The residential concentrations of the Gujarati- and of the Hindi-speaking serve as an index of high- and low-income areas respectively. Only the Indians, among the three Non-European groups, have secured an appreciable footing on the slopes of the central ridge, and on the sea front north of the Umgeni River.

The distribution of the African population includes domestic servants, and employees in barracks and compounds

---

[1] The City Council of Durban has established a relatively high-class housing scheme for Coloureds at Sparks Road, within the Inland Transitional zone, west of the Central Berea Ridge.

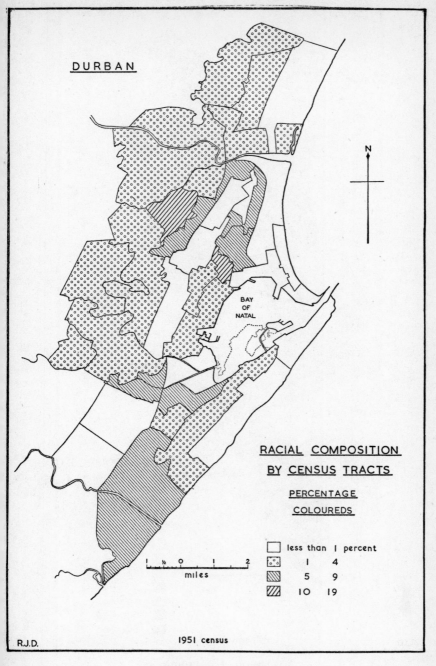

DURBAN

N

BAY
OF
NATAL

RACIAL COMPOSITION
BY CENSUS TRACTS

PERCENTAGE

COLOUREDS

	less than 1 percent
	1 4
	5 9
	10 19

1 ½ 0 1 2
miles

R.J.D.

1951 census

FIGURE 17: COLOUREDS

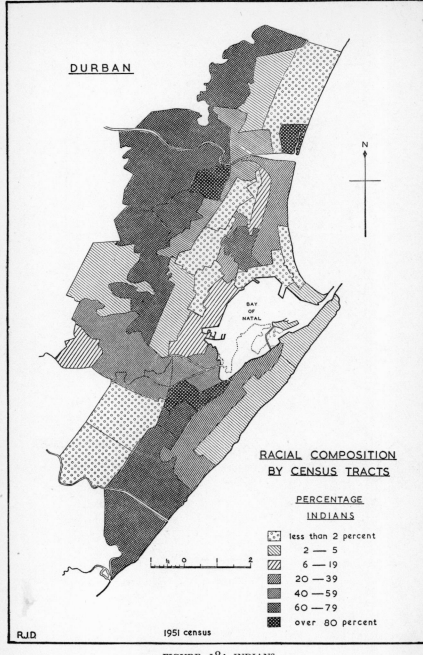

DURBAN

N

BAY
OF
NATAL

RACIAL COMPOSITION
BY CENSUS TRACTS

PERCENTAGE
INDIANS

less than 2 percent
2 — 5
6 — 19
20 — 39
40 — 59
60 — 79
over 80 percent

R.J.D.

1951 census

FIGURE 18: INDIANS

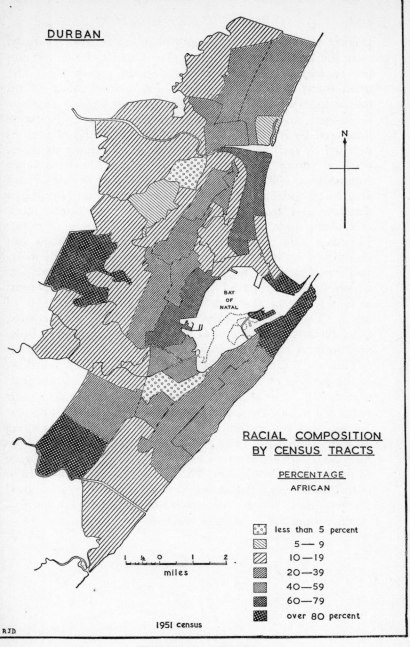

DURBAN

N

BAY
OF
NATAL

RACIAL COMPOSITION
BY CENSUS TRACTS

PERCENTAGE
AFRICAN

less than 5 percent
5 — 9
10 — 19
20 — 39
40 — 59
60 — 79
over 80 percent

1 ½ 0 1 2
miles

1951 census

RJD

FIGURE 19: AFRICANS

(Figure 19, p. 141). The shading is not so strongly contrasted as in the European and Indian distributions, demonstrating the general dependence on the African population. The main tracts with concentrations of African families are on the periphery, particularly in the Lamont Location on the south-west, and in Cato Manor on the west. This is a zone inhabited by high proportions of Christians and of persons married by civil or religious rites, or simply living together. With a young age structure and a fairly balanced sex composition, it is sharply differentiated from the Sea Front and the Alluvial Flats, in which lives an African population characterized by migrant labour, high masculinity rates, lobola marriage, ancestor-worship and affiliation to minor Christian and separatist sects. Generally, Africans are established either in accommodation provided for them by their employers or the City Council, or in accommodation which they have found for themselves—usually the most unsatisfactory of shack dwellings in the least desirable of areas. They are not involved in ecological competition, but have settled for the most part on land allocated to them and on land rejected by other groups.

This, then, is the residential distribution, in broad outline, of the peoples of Durban. There is a measure of 'natural' segregation which gives to the different physiographic regions a distinctive social character, based partly on race. Income and occupation create further differentiation along class divisions within the racial groups; they also cut across race boundaries and bring together people of different race in the same area of living. This 'natural' ecological pattern of incomplete segregation is now to be replaced by a planned resegregation, which will secure maximum racial 'purity' in the residential districts of Durban.

CHAPTER VI

SEGREGATION, PURE AND APPLIED

THE distinction between pure ('natural' or voluntary) segregation and applied (planned or compulsory) segregation may be clear in theory: it is often ambiguous when related to a concrete situation. If, for example, we examine broad legislative trends in Natal, we can readily distinguish between the voluntary segregation of the past, and the compulsory segregation of the Group Areas Act. The distinction becomes blurred, however, when applied to the specific situation of ecological competition between the Europeans and Indians of Durban. At the ideological level we find that the demand for compulsory segregation often rests on precisely the same assumption as the plea for voluntary segregation, while, in practice, both compulsion and co-operation are woven into the pattern of segregation. On the one hand, there was a good deal of compulsion in the voluntary segregation of the past, and, on the other hand, it seems likely that co-operation will be necessary to the compulsory segregation of the future.

The Indian 'Penetration' Commissions provide a convenient point for the study of segregation in Durban, since they mark the final phase between the more permissive procedures of the past and the restrictive legislation which culminated in the Group Areas Act. The first 'Penetration' Commission was appointed in May 1940, shortly after the outbreak of the Second World War, in response to a mounting agitation against the Indians. Its terms of reference were to inquire into the extent to which Indians had, subsequent to the 1st January 1927, acquired, or commenced occupation of, sites for trading or for residential purposes in predominantly European areas in the Provinces of Natal and the Transvaal.[1] It was also instructed to investigate the reasons for such occupation or acquisition.

The Commission's second term of reference, the inquiry as to the reasons for Indian movement into predominantly European areas, implies that any deviation from racial segregation requires explanation, or, in other words, that racial segregation is 'normal', 'natural'. The assumption is that people of the same race instinctively desire to live together. Thus, the Durban City Council complained to the First 'Penetration' Commission that Indians had acted in violation of the *communal instinct* implanted in all human beings, since they had scattered their acquisitions, instead of centralizing them in a particular area,[2] where, that is to say, they would have lived with their own kind.

The acceptance of a natural-instinct theory of segregation by Europeans is intelligible in terms of a European interest in race segregation. It explains the European desire to live apart, and may provide justification for compulsion. Since segregation is 'natural', as shown by the extent of segregation reported in many cities, deviation from segregation is reprehensible, unnatural: hence it is right to restrain these unnatural practices by compulsory segregation. One of the functions then of the 'natural theory of segregation', for Europeans, is to provide a rationale for compulsory segregation.

There are some curious aspects to this argument, particu-

---

[1] The date 1st January 1927 was chosen because the Cape Town Agreement of that year, between the Governments of India and of South Africa, inaugurated, or was designed to inaugurate, a new era in Indian-European relations (page 28, Chapter I). The Cape Town Agreement combined a scheme of assisted emigration for Indians wishing to return to India with the obligation to uplift the considerable number of Indians who would remain part of the permanent population of South Africa. Calpin, in *Indians in South Africa*, gives an extended account of the Cape Town Agreement and of the Penetration Commissions. The description 'penetration' was not used in the terms of reference, but was coined by the European public.

[2] U.G. No. 39–41, p. 72.

larly when we reflect on the artificial character of the urban
environment, the many social restraints on the expression
of natural impulses, and the extent to which 'nature' is
socially suspect. Moreover, the identification of the 'natural'
with the 'socially' desirable is not consistently drawn by the
advocates of compulsory segregation. When Indians in
Durban did, in fact, concentrate their purchases in a
particular European area, Block AL on the lower slopes of
the central ridge, Europeans did not interpret this as a
'natural' expression of a 'communal instinct' and hence
socially desirable.[1] On the contrary, they were more firmly
resolved than ever on compulsory segregation, and so deep
was their resentment of what they regarded as an invasion
of their prerogatives that the Second 'Penetration' Commission was appointed to investigate the matter. The
reliance on the natural-instinct theory varies with circumstances. It is not a basic assumption, but a weapon in
a conflict of interests between a dominant group seeking to
impose segregation and a resisting subordinate group.

We would, therefore, expect Non-European leaders to
reject the assumption that racial segregation is natural.
This is, however, not consistently the case. Thus, at the
Durban hearings of the First 'Penetration' Commission,
one of the Indian leaders declared 'that natural causes—
the causes of the affinity of religion, culture and race—will
always prevail and will always group people of one race,
one colour, and one religion into certain areas. Therefore,
it is not difficult to visualize, from what has been human
experience all over the world—even in the East, in towns
like Singapore, Bombay, and elsewhere—that people of one
race, one colour and one religion, will always group into

---

[1] The Town Clerk of the City of Durban declared in September 1953, at
the hearings by the Group Areas Board, that the Indians in Block AL were
partly responsible for the Group Areas legislation (*Natal Daily News*, 3rd
September 1953). These purchases in Block AL were an extension of the
Indian area of settlement in the Old Borough, based on tract 13 on the lower
slopes of the central ridge and tract 18 in the Alluvial Flats.

K

certain areas.'[1] The conclusion drawn from this assumption is that, since segregation is natural, there will be so few cases of deviation that compulsion is not necessary. The function of the assumption, for Indians, is therefore to allay the fear of the Europeans, and to provide a basis for *de facto* segregation through voluntary co-operation.

Proceeding from the assumption that race segregation is instinctive, deviation has to be explained, and again the explanations vary with the interests of the group concerned. From the point of view of the European, the explanation may be sought in some defect within the Indian community or in the Indian character. 'Penetration' is *prima facie* evidence of guilt: representatives of local authorities and individual witnesses at the First 'Penetration' Commission took up the attitude that the onus was on the Indians to explain why they had 'penetrated' predominantly European areas. One witness suggested that penetration was 'a gesture of defiance' against the policy of segregation, while the Durban City Council initially advanced the tentative explanation that the reason was psychological, rather than material—the desire to demonstrate equality in all respects with the European.[2]

An alternative approach by Europeans is to regard 'penetration', not as a deviation from the communal instinct, but, on the contrary, as an expression of it. Indians are assumed to have a highly developed, indeed over-developed, communal instinct—this is in fact a common allegation—and 'penetration' is thus interpreted as part of a sinister movement for the invasion and acquisition of the City of Durban, a tentacle of Indian Imperialism. It is clear that it is difficult for Indians to behave correctly in the eyes of Europeans—the same acts of 'penetration' may be a deviation from the communal instinct, or its sinister product.

Conversely, those Indian leaders who subscribe to the

---

[1] *Report of the First Indian 'Penetration' Commission*, pp. 73–4.   [2] Ibid., pp. 72–3.

'natural' theory of segregation, must seek the reasons for 'penetration' in forces outside the Indian community. They charge the authorities with the deliberate neglect of Indian areas, and the failure to provide opportunities for good homes in well-serviced districts. They point also to the limitations on occupational choice and on avenues of investment for Indians in the country as a whole. But for these factors, they declare, there would be little or no Indian 'penetration'. The causes of Indian 'penetration' are to be found in the unjust policies of European authorities.

This reliance by representatives of both European and Indian groups on 'communal instinct' brings together the concepts of compulsory segregation and voluntary segregation as variations on a single theme. The difference between *de facto* segregation through voluntary co-operation and *de jure* segregation by compulsion becomes exceedingly subtle, as can be seen in the activities of the Lawrence Committee, appointed about the same time as the First 'Penetration' Commission. The task of the Indian members of the Lawrence Committee was to persuade Indians to refrain from buying or occupying properties in European areas, while the European members, representing the Durban City Council, undertook to dissuade Europeans in European areas from selling to Indians. If the activities of the Lawrence Committee had been successful, the only difference between voluntary segregation achieved in this way and compulsory segregation would have been in the nature of the sanctions— group pressure instead of legal pressure: and in the psychological consequences—the honour of the Indian community might have been saved by the rationalization that it acted as a freely contracting agent in the interests of racial harmony.

In fact, there is no valid ground for the assumption of a 'communal instinct' or an inborn predisposition to racial segregation. The acceptance of this assumption is an index of racial antipathy, not of scientific validity. Indeed, the premise of a 'communal instinct' removes the problem from the field of scientific inquiry. Certainly, affinity in language, culture and race is a major factor in the segregation of groups, but the 'communal-instinct' theory over-emphasizes the importance of this affinity by excluding the highly significant role of the political and economic structure of the society.

The main inquiry of the First 'Penetration' Commission was directed to the extent of segregation in the provinces of the Transvaal and Natal, but within the narrow perspective prescribed by the Government. It was limited to segregation between Europeans and Indians, which is adequate, however, for our purposes, since only the Indians seriously competed with Europeans for the land of Durban. Moreover, the terms of reference were defined essentially from a European point of view—the extent of 'penetration' by Indians, and not 'penetration' generally. There must have been considerable 'penetration' by Europeans into the predominantly Non-European Added Areas of Durban.[1]

The problem of 'penetration' in the Transvaal was primarily a problem of occupation, since the acquisition of ownership of land by Indians was virtually prohibited. Under these restricted conditions, we would expect 'penetration' to be of minor proportions, as the Commission indeed found. In Natal, on the other hand, there were no legislative restrictions on either the acquisition or occupation of land, save in the Northern districts; yet, under these apparently free conditions, the extent of penetration was very little greater than in the Transvaal. The average number of subdivisions acquired *per annum* in the unproclaimed areas of the Transvaal was twenty-five, in Natal outside Durban twenty-three (or twenty-nine including agricultural land), and in Durban thirty-six.[2] In fact, there was *relatively* far less 'penetration' in Natal, since the Indian population in

---

[1] The Commission did not doubt that the greater part of the Added Areas was predominantly Non-European in 1927. Ibid., p. 71.
[2] Ibid., p. 68.

Natal was seven times as large as the Transvaal Indian population, and since 'penetration' took the form of acquisition, as well as of occupation. It is of considerable interest that the restrictive conditions in the Transvaal should promote relatively greater 'penetration' than conditions of voluntary segregation. It is only partly explained by the predominantly trading character of the Transvaal Indian population as compared with the largely labouring population of Natal.

The 'penetration', moreover, was not the deliberate invasion which the term suggests, but simply the acquisition or occupation of trading and residential sites in predominantly European areas. In determining the racial character of an area, the Commission emphasized the racial composition of the residents, save in Durban where the City Council argued that ownership was the correct test. Its reasons were that occupation tends to follow ownership, so that residential segregation requires the segregation of ownership. The City Council, therefore, provided information in respect of ownership only, and virtually limited the inquiry to the investigation of residential sites in the Old Borough. The number of trading sites in the European areas of Durban, acquired by Indians after 1927, was negligible, since the authorities had secured effective segregation in trade by control over the issue of licences. Thus, the main issue before the 'Penetration' Commission was the ownership by Indians of residential sites in the European areas of the Old Borough.[1] The 'penetration' in Durban, reported by the Commission, refers to these acquisitions.

The Commission defined the European areas of the Old Borough negatively as those which were not predominantly Indian-owned in 1927, and demarcated seven areas, in

---

[1] The fate of the so-called 'Pretoria Agreement' of 1944 is further evidence of the importance attached to ownership by the Europeans of Durban. This agreement, between representatives of the Indian community and the Prime Minister, made provision for the control of occupation only, and proved entirely unacceptable to the European population of Durban.

extent about 204 acres, as predominantly Indian-owned in 1927. The seven areas lie almost entirely in the Alluvial Flats. Some are near the centre of the town, opposite railway workshops, or bounded by a cemetery and railway line; densely developed, partly blighted. One section consists of innumerable small shops with living-rooms above, and honeycombed by narrow arcades. There is invasion by industry, markets, bus-ranks, depots, locations. They are precisely the areas in which we would have expected a relatively poor community to settle. More than half the sites acquired by Indians, subsequent to January 1927, were in adjacent areas, some of which had already become predominantly Indian-owned before the appointment of the First 'Penetration' Commission, while the remaining acquisitions were scattered throughout the Old Borough. In the great majority of cases the new owners were not in occupation of their properties.

The facts did not indicate a planned invasion of European areas. The Commission concluded that the desire to live among one's own people is a natural instinct in human beings, and that Indians were no different in this respect from others.[1] It dismissed 'gestures of defiance' and the demonstration of equality as insignificant factors, though conceding that they might account for a few cases of 'penetration', and found the main cause in the desire of the Indian community for good investments. An important contributory cause was that the areas in the Alluvial Flats had ceased to be attractive to Europeans, and, as they moved out into the more desirable modern suburbs, properties became available to Indian purchasers. Other contributory causes, reported by the Commission, were the effects of the Cape Town Agreement,[2]

---

[1] Ibid., p. 73.
[2] See Chapter I, page 28. Indian representatives had argued that the 'upliftment' clauses in the Cape Town Agreement of 1927 gave security to the Indians by recognizing them as part of the permanent population, and encouraged them to invest their money in South Africa and to conform to Western standards of life, thus creating a demand for more and better houses.

the increase in Indian population, and the lack of decent housing and of general civic amenities in some of the predominantly Indian areas. The Commission did not find proven the charge of deliberate neglect of Indian areas by the City Council, though it ventured the judicious comment that refusal or postponement of calls on the civic purse is perhaps less likely if the consequent disappointment can be expressed through the ballot box.[1]

There was nothing in these findings to provide political argument for restrictive legislation, in contrast to the findings of the Second Indian 'Penetration' Commission, appointed in February 1943 specifically to report on recent acquisitions in the Old Borough of Durban. This Commission found that there were 326 cases of 'penetration' between October 1940 and February 1943, and that the purchase price paid for these sites did not fall far short of the total amount paid during the previous thirteen years covered by the first commission.[2] A sensational aspect of the report was a map of purchases, concentrated in Block AL on the lower slopes of the central ridge, which gave the appearance of planned 'penetration'. The terms of reference did not include reasons for 'penetration', but the Commissioner suggested the following: money becoming available for investment as

[1] *Report of the First Indian 'Penetration' Commission*, p. 70. The reasons given by the Commission for penetration in the Transvaal have relevance also for the situation in Durban. The Commission first of all disposed of a number of arguments by European witnesses. In view of the restrictions on Indian investment in the Transvaal, the Commission expressed its amazement at the complaint that Indians sent their savings to India. It commented on the cruel dilemma of the Transvaal Indian, accused of acting to the detriment of public health when living on his trading premises, and of 'penetration' when he sought a home away from his business. It dismissed the theory that the first Indian 'penetration' of an area caused an exodus of the European population, and thus made possible a large-scale invasion, but concluded that the areas had ceased to be attractive to Europeans, and that degeneration of the areas and the European exodus preceded Indian 'penetration'. The main cause of 'penetration' was found in 'the normal desire among Indians to acquire wealth', with subsidiary causes in their limited occupational opportunities and the encouragement of the Cape Town Agreement (ibid., pp. 42–4).
[2] *Report of the Second Indian 'Penetration' (Durban) Commission*, U.G. 21/1943, p. 4.

a result of the restriction of trade during the war; the reluctance of many Indians to lend out money on interest, and their preference for investment in immovable property; misinterpretation of the findings of the First 'Penetration' Commission, and a possible anxiety to pass through the door while it was still ajar.[1]

The Government immediately responded to the report of the Second 'Penetration' Commission by restrictive legislation in the form of the Trading and Occupation of Land (Transvaal and Natal) Restriction Act of 1943, the so-called 'Pegging Act'. This maintained the *status quo* in Durban by prohibiting changes of ownership or occupation between Europeans and Indians, save with ministerial consent. Conceived as a temporary measure, the 'Pegging Act' was followed in 1946 by the Asiatic Land Tenure and Indian Representation Act, which incorporated the general restrictions of the 'Pegging Act', save in specially exempted areas, where Indians were free to buy and occupy land. The Group Areas Act passed shortly after, in 1950, re-introduced control over inter-racial changes of ownership and occupation throughout the whole of Durban, that is in both the exempted and unexempted areas. Since, therefore, material changes in the racial composition of the residential areas of Durban could not have taken place between the 'Penetration' commissions and the 1951 Census, we can use the Census figures as a rough guide to the extent of segregation under the more permissive procedures of the past.

Our measure of segregation between Europeans and Indians is based on the race of residents, not of owners, in the 36 census tracts of Durban, since this is the only reliable information we have of racial distribution. In Table XXXV, following the 'segregation index' method investigated by

[1] Ibid., pp. 5–6. In tract 18, on the Alluvial Flats, the Greyville Race Course lies between the predominantly Indian areas, and the European areas on the Central Berea Ridge. Instead of leaping this barrier, Indian purchasers flanked it by the movement into Block AL in tract 9.

Duncan and Davis,[1] we have ranked the tracts on the basis
of the ratio of Indians to Europeans, so that the tract with
the highest ratio is ranked first—Columns 1, 2 and 3.

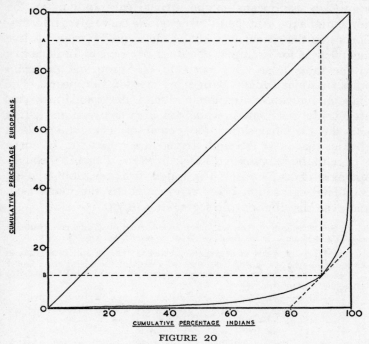

FIGURE 20

SEGREGATION CURVE FOR SEGREGATION OF INDIANS FROM
EUROPEANS, DURBAN, 1951 (CENSUS TRACT BASIS)

Columns 4 and 5 give the percentage of Indians and
Europeans respectively in each tract, and Columns 6 and 7
the cumulated percentages. Thus, reading Columns 6 and 7,
we see that 12·22 per cent of Indians, but only 0·04 per cent
of Europeans, live in tracts 29 and 28, or, again, that 89·84

[1] O. D. Duncan and B. Davis, *The Chicago Urban Analysis Project* (University
of Chicago, December 1953). See also O. D. Duncan and B. Duncan, 'A
Methodological Analysis of Segregation Indexes', *American Sociological Review*,
vol. XX (April 1955), pp. 210–17.

per cent of Indians live in the same 17 tracts as 10·86 per cent of Europeans.

The cumulated percentages are presented graphically in Figure 20, Europeans on the vertical axis, Indians on the horizontal axis. Any point taken on the curve gives information as to the extent to which Indians and Europeans live together: as for example, about 40 per cent of Indians live in the same areas as 1 per cent of Europeans, or again 60 per cent of Indians with 2 per cent of Europeans. The diagonal indicates a situation in which Indians and Europeans are evenly distributed, while the area between the curve and the diagonal shows the extent of segregation. It is obvious that there is a high degree of segregation; the curve is close to the maximum distance from the diagonal throughout most of its course. The index of segregation[1] is 0·91, complete segregation being represented by the index 1·00, and even distribution (no segregation) by 0.

[1] By the technique of the segregation index based on Gini's concentration ratio (The Chicago Urban Analysis Report, op. cit., pp. 19–25).

Computation of Index of Segregation between Indians and Europeans in Durban, Census 1951, Using Ten Selected Points of the Segregation Curve (X representing Cumulative Percentage Indians, Y representing Cumulative Percentage Europeans).

	X_i	Y	$X_{i-1}Y_i$	X_iY_{i-1}
1	0·00	0·00	0·00	0·00
2	12·22	0·04	0·00	0·00
3	30·11	0·51	6·23	1·20
4	45·69	1·12	33·72	23·30
5	70·59	3·45	157·63	79·06
6	89·84	10·86	766·61	309·95
7	98·88	30·87	2,773·36	1,073·84
8	99·47	48·43	4,788·76	3,070·64
9	99·79	69·16	6,879·35	4,832·83
10	100·00	100·00	9,979·00	6,916·00
			25,384·66	16,306·82

$$\text{Index of segregation} = (\Sigma X_{i-1}Y_i - \Sigma X_iY_{i-1})$$
$$= \frac{25384 \cdot 66 - 16306 \cdot 82}{10,000}$$
$$= 0 \cdot 91$$

TABLE XXXV

SEGREGATION OF INDIANS FROM EUROPEANS IN DURBAN BY OCCUPANCY OF CENSUS TRACTS: 1951 CENSUS

1 Rank Order	2 Census Tract No.	3 Ratio % Indians : % Europeans	4 % Indians	5 % Europeans	6 Cumulative Percentages Indians	7 Europeans
1	29	371·00	11·13	0·03	11·13	0·03
2	28	109·00	1·09	0·01	12·22	0·04
3	24	68·00	0·68	0·01	12·90	0·05
4	5	54·33	1·63	0·03	14·53	0·08
5	22	47·88	7·66	0·16	22·19	0·24
6	6	29·33	7·92	0·27	30·11	0·51
7	21	26·29	6·31	0·24	36·42	0·75
8	30	25·44	4·07	0·16	40·49	0·91
9	7	24·76	5·20	0·21	45·69	1·12
10	23	14·78	12·57	0·85	58·26	1·97
11	18	8·77	9·12	1·04	67·38	3·01
12	33	7·30	3·21	0·44	70·59	3·45
13	4	5·76	3·40	0·59	73·99	4·04
14	1	5·69	3·36	0·59	77·35	4·63
15	20	3·01	7·61	2·53	84·96	7·16
16	27	2·09	1·42	0·68	86·38	7·84
17	13	1·15	3·46	3·02	89·84	10·86
18	26	1·02	3·91	3·85	93·75	14·71
19	16	0·51	0·69	1·36	94·44	16·07
20	31	0·47	2·25	4·78	96·69	20·85
21	9	0·42	0·70	1·67	97·39	22·52
22	36	0·21	0·23	1·07	97·62	23·59
23	8	0·19	1·08	5·42	98·70	29·01
24	35	0·12	*0·00(4)	0·04	98·70	29·05
25	25	0·10	0·18	1·82	98·88	30·87
26	32	0·05	0·12	2·27	99·00	33·14
27	2	0·04	0·17	3·85	99·17	36·99
28	14	0·03	0·22	7·46	99·39	44·45
29	10	0·02	0·08	3·98	99·47	48·43
30	3	0·02	0·10	5·60	99·57	54·03
31	12	0·02	0·16	10·58	99·73	64·61
32	11	0·01	0·06	4·55	99·79	69·16
33	19	0·01	0·08	9·17	99·87	78·33
34	17	0·01	0·09	10·58	99·96	88·91
35	15	0·00	0·04	8·55	100·00	97·46
36	34	0·00	*0·00(3)	2·54	100·00	100·00
			100·00	100·00		

* For the purpose of working out the ratio % Indians : % Europeans, these figures are significant to three decimal places.

The vertical distance between the point on the curve farthest from the diagonal and the diagonal itself (AB in Figure 20) gives a measure of the percentage of the Indian population which would have to be moved in order to achieve an even distribution of Europeans and Indians— that is, no segregation. The relevant percentage is 79·04.[1] Or we can phrase our conclusion in terms of the minimum movement of Europeans and Indians necessary for complete segregation in the census tracts. This would be a movement of 14·71 per cent Europeans out of the first eighteen tracts listed in Table XXXV, and a corresponding movement of 6·25 per cent Indians into these eighteen areas. Complete segregation could also be secured by moving 10·86 per cent Europeans from, and 10·16 per cent Indians into, the first seventeen areas listed, but this would involve a slightly larger movement of population.

Comparison of the index of segregation between Europeans and Indians in Durban, and indexes calculated by Duncan and Davis in the United States of America, can only be very rough, but it is of interest that the indexes of the segregation of non-whites for 60 large American cities ranged from 0·60 to 0·95, except for one suburban city with an index of 0·45.[2] In other words, Durban would be ranked among the cities with the most extreme segregation. Indeed the index of 0·91 for Durban understates the extent of segregation in comparison with the American cities, since the census tracts used in this study have a much larger population on the average than the census tracts in the United States. There is considerable segregation also within the census tracts in which both Europeans and Indians live, so that the amount of residential intermingling must be very small indeed.

Indians are also highly segregated from Africans (the

---

[1] See discussion by Duncan and Davis of the Coefficient of Dissimilarity, op. cit., p. 22.
[2] Ibid., p. 87. Comparisons are affected by the proportion of non-whites to whites, by their spatial distribution, and by the methods used in defining the spatial units.

index is 0·81, excluding domestic servants in private house-holds). The index of segregation between Coloureds and Europeans is higher (0·84). In the case of Europeans and Africans, we have information as to the distribution of domestic servants in private households, and not of all domestic servants. The index, excluding African servants in private households, is 0·81: excluding all African domestic servants, it must be very close to total segregation. Only Coloureds and Indians live together in the same areas to an appreciable extent.

Our index of segregation between Europeans and Indians, though based on the 1951 Census, gives an approximate measure of the extent of segregation prior to the imposition of compulsory segregation by law. There can be no doubt that it was extremely high, particularly when we bear in mind that the first indentured Indians reached Durban in 1860, that Durban has since grown from a small trading settlement to a large industrial and commercial city, and that many Indian families have lived in Durban for longer than a large percentage of European families. It would be superficial to explain this segregation entirely in terms of a 'communal instinct'. In addition to cultural and racial affinity, economic factors were most important, above all the extreme poverty of the indentured Indians, which persists to this day among many of their descendants, as we have shown in our analysis of income distribution. Most Indians were obliged to settle in areas of low cost, on the Alluvial Flats near marshy ground, on the outskirts beyond municipal control, or in blighted central areas, areas which Europeans had vacated. The growth of a wealthy trading class is a recent development (though some of the early Indian immigrants, the 'passenger' as distinct from the indentured, arrived with capital), and there was probably little desire to demon-strate status by the acquisition of homes high up on the Berea.

But economic factors and cultural affinity do not fully explain the segregation. In the last resort, it rested also on deliberate policy and indirect compulsion. At the level of municipal policy, barrack accommodation and housing projects were on a segregated, not on an inter-racial, basis. In 1922 the City Council acquired the power, when selling or leasing land, to reserve ownership or occupation for a particular racial group, and it used this power to reserve land for Europeans.[1] The European residents themselves assisted in this process. In the subdivision of old estates on the Central Berea Ridge, as a result of the increasing levy of municipal rates, restrictive clauses were often inserted, while neighbours sometimes entered into deeds of restraint to ensure that adjoining properties would not be sold to Indians.[2] In consequence, many areas in Durban became reserved for Europeans only. Where there were no restrictive conditions, pressure of public opinion might prevent private sales to Indians, and the Building Societies exercised some control by their loan policies.

The driving force behind these restrictions was the intense hostility of Europeans to Indians.[3] It acted as a most powerful indirect compulsion. Its strength is shown by the fact that a major European agitation against Indian 'penetration' arose at a time when there were actually few cases of 'penetration', insufficient in the opinion of a judicial

[1] *Report of the First 'Penetration' Commission*, op. cit., p. 8. The Indian community persistently refused to accept transfer subject to restrictions which they regarded as designed to bring about segregation. See Chapter I, page 33.

[2] We are indebted to Mr I. Geshen, estate agent of Durban, for these comments.

[3] Evidence of this is to be found in the attitude of European witnesses before the 'penetration' commissions and in the history of anti-Indian agitation in the 1940s. It is shown also by the double-edged character of some of the accusations, so that any form of behaviour would be culpable. A further illustration of this may be of interest. At one time we proposed to investigate the allegation that Indians bought homes on *street corners*, so as to drive out Europeans from the remaining houses in the block. We abandoned this project when we were assured that Indian policy was to acquire houses in the *middle of the street* with the same purpose in mind.

commission to give cause for alarm. This demonstrates the nature of the non-legal sanctions against the Indians. Theoretically, they were free to buy and occupy land where they pleased in those areas of the city not subject to restrictive conditions, that is to say, they were free to buy and occupy land in a large part of the city. In practice, in the Old Borough at any rate, there was pressure on them to concentrate in sections abandoned by Europeans. The sanction for 'voluntary' segregation was the threat of compulsory segregation, and it was carried out at the first substantial deviation from 'voluntary' segregation in the less desirable sections of the Old Borough.

If 'voluntary' segregation in Durban had a strong measure of compulsion, it is possible that the compulsory segregation of the Group Areas Act may be more voluntary than it appears. This is indeed the contention of the Durban City Council.

The Group Areas Act[1] radically extends the control over private property. It removes the limitations which vested rights imposed on the planner's freedom to create new patterns of segregation, and thus provides the means for retrospective planning. Rights of ownership are subordinated to racial zoning, and conventional teaching in regard to the 'sanctity' of private property must now be sharply modified. The 'secularization' of ownership goes far beyond the powers previously vested in the authorities to expropriate land and buildings for public projects or for slum clearance. These powers are exercised in exceptional circumstances, while racial zoning is now an ordinary routine of Town Planning. Racial criteria restrict, much more radically than in the past, the right of the individual to acquire the ownership of land

---

[1] Act No. 41 of 1950, as amended by the Group Areas Amendment Act No. 65 of 1952, the Group Areas Amendment Act No. 6 of 1955, the Group Areas Further Amendment Act No. 68 of 1955, the Group Areas Amendment Act No. 29 of 1956, and the Group Areas Amendment Act No. 57 of 1957. All these provisions have now been consolidated in the Group Areas Act No. 77 of 1957.

and buildings, while the rights attached to ownership itself, including the right of testamentary disposition and the right of occupation, are similarly restricted, even where ownership was acquired many years before the passing of the Group Areas Act.

Initially, the departure from established principles was all the more marked because of the lack of provision for compensation against loss. On the contrary, compliance with the Act was, and is, sanctioned by heavy penalties of imprisonment or fine or both, regardless of the losses the individual property owner might sustain. It was not until 1955 that the Government, stimulated by public agitation and the insistence of the Durban City Council,[1] introduced the Group Areas Development Act, which provides the necessary machinery for compensation.

There is, however, still no obligation on the Government to find accommodation for persons displaced; the availability of alternative accommodation must be taken into consideration, when Group Areas are proclaimed, but there is no compulsion whatever to do anything arising out of this consideration. Indeed, the phrase 'alternative accommodation' appears to be interpreted as an area where accommodation could be built, and not as actual accommodation. The Development Act itself makes further inroads into the rights of ownership, by procedures for regulating the sale price of property in the open market, and by expropriation of properties under a system of public acquisition for the development of Group Areas. The acceptance by Europeans of such revolutionary changes in the traditionally sacred rights of ownership indicates their conviction that the provisions of the Group Areas Act would be applied against Non-Europeans, and for the benefit of Europeans.

---

[1] The Durban City Council maintained close liaison with the Government, and contributed substantially to the shaping of the amending legislation, as indeed to Group Areas legislation generally and to the theory of racial zoning.

The controls provided by the Group Areas Act extend not only over the ownership of property but also over its occupation, and are exceedingly varied in character. In the case of ownership, the racial *status quo* may be 'pegged' by the prohibition of inter-racial changes in ownership; or the racial *status quo* may be profoundly altered by compulsory change. So, too, occupation may be 'pegged', no change in the race of the occupant of premises being permitted, save with ministerial consent; only Indians, for example, could move into a home previously occupied by an Indian family. Or the occupancy of premises may be controlled by the requirement that the race of the occupier must be the same as that of the owner. Or change in occupancy may be compelled by the reservation of an area for a particular racial group. The controls over occupation have been extended to include control over a wide variety of inter-racial contacts by a recent amendment (Section 1 (4) of Act 57 of 1957), which empowers the Governor-General to apply the provisions of the Group Areas Act to any person present on land or premises 'for a substantial period of time or for the purpose of attending any public entertainment or partaking of any refreshment at a place where refreshments are served or as a member of or guest in any club as if his presence constituted occupation of such land or premises'. And the Governor-General has now exercised these powers over inter-racial contact in respect of cinemas, restaurants, tea-rooms and clubs (Proclamation No. 333 of 1957).

Control over trading and employment is linked, almost incidentally, with the controls over ownership and occupation. Effective segregation in trade may readily be secured by the simple requirement that the person in control of the business must belong to a racial group entitled to occupy the premises. In this way the informal procedures used in the past by the Durban City Council are now systematized and effectively sanctioned. Similarly, control over inter-racial

L

contacts of employment is secured by the general requirement that, save under special permit, only persons of the qualified racial group may occupy land or premises in Group Areas. Employees of Government and statutory bodies were exempted from this requirement under the Act, and a broad exemption was granted by the Governor-General, who at the same time specifically excluded certain categories of employee (Proclamations 328 and 329 of 1957). Thus, domestic servants are exempt only in Group Areas reserved for occupation by white persons; no white person may be employed in non-white areas, nor may any disqualified persons be employed in managerial, supervisory, or senior professional and technical posts, or as charge-hands.

All these controls are based on racial criteria, the racial groups established by the Act being White, Native and Coloured.[1] The Governor-General has the power to subdivide the Native (African) and Coloured Groups, but not the White, on the basis of ethnic, linguistic, cultural or other characteristics. An Indian, Chinese, and, in the Cape, a Malay Group, have been established as subdivisions of the Coloureds by the Governor-General's fiat. The Natives are not yet subdivided under the Group Areas Act, but the Minister of Native Affairs has issued an instruction to urban administrators that Natives must be settled residentially according to their ethnic origin. Three main linguistic groups, Nguni, Sotho and Other are suggested, with linguistic sub-groups if numbers permit.[2]

[1] The conventional racial classification in South Africa is European, Coloured, Asiatic and Native. Some Indian political leaders regard the omission of Asiatics or Indians from the race classification of the Group Areas Act as an expression of Government policy, namely, the categorization of Indians as an alien and outlandish element, which must therefore be expatriated. (See Dr G. M. Naicker's paper, 'The Group Areas Act and its effects on the Indian people', submitted to a conference convened by the Natal Indian Congress in May 1956.)

[2] Paper delivered by J. E. Mathewson, Director of Non-European Affairs, Benoni, to the South African Institute of Race Relations (Johannesburg, RR 227/55, dated 23rd December 1955, pp. 21 et seq.). The Municipality of Benoni has subdivided the Native population of Daveytown into eight linguistic groups.

The method of applying the controls over the racial ecology of a city is through the proclamation of areas of different types by the Governor-General on the advice of the Minister of Interior. These types of areas are as follows:

(1) *The Controlled Area*

Inter-racial change of ownership is prohibited, and the occupier must be of the same race group as the owner. Certain categories are exempt from the restrictions on occupation, as for example employees of the State, and domestic servants.[1]

(2) *The Specified Area*

This pegs the *status quo*: inter-racial changes in ownership or occupation are prohibited.

(3) *The Defined Area*

Within Specified Areas, provision may be made to increase the control of occupation, by the requirement that the Minister of the Interior shall determine which group is entitled to occupy vacant land or new, reconstructed or extended buildings. In this way the racial composition of an area, especially of an undeveloped area, can be influenced.

(4) *Proposed Group Area for Occupation and/or Ownership*

The Governor-General defines an area which he proposes at some future date, unspecified, to reserve for the occupation and/or ownership of a particular group. It is a declaration of intention, and in the interim period provides control over land use and the subdivision of land, while serving as notice that members of certain

---

[1] Provision is made for what the Minister of Interior describes as an Open Area, that is a portion of a Controlled Area not subject to the condition that the occupier must be of the same race as the owner.

race groups will become disqualified and had best look around for new homes and trading premises.

Similar control over land use and subdivision, but with restriction also on sale and occupation, may be applied to *Border Strips*—that is to say buffer zones or no-man's-land between Group Areas, where no natural or other barriers exist.

(5) *Group Area for Occupation*

This is the reservation of an area for occupation by a particular group from a specified date. At least one year's notice must be given. Again, certain temporary occupants, including domestic servants at the discretion of the Governor-General, are exempt. The right of occupancy is divorced from that of ownership, so that a disqualified person may continue in ownership of a property, but not be free to occupy it.

(6) *Group Area for Ownership*

On the reservation of an area for the ownership of a particular race group, members of other races are disqualified from acquiring ownership of immovable property in the area. A disqualified person who owned land in the area, prior to its establishment as a Group Area, may continue to hold it until his death, when transfer must be made to a qualified person.[1] If, for example, an Indian acquired a home in an area subsequently reserved for White Ownership, and he bequeaths it to his sons and daughters, he is deemed to have bequeathed, not the property, but the nett proceeds of its sale to a White person. In effect then, the acquisition of ownership by qualified persons will be completed, at the latest, when the last surviving disqualified owner

[1] Since ownership may be expropriated under the Group Areas Development Act No. 69 of 1955, the above safeguard provided by the Group Areas Act is at the discretion of the Group Areas Development Board.

dies. Occupation of each property must be by a person of the same race as the owner.

(7) Group Area for Ownership and Occupation

Both ownership and occupation are restricted to one race group, but a member of another race group who already owns land in the area may continue to hold it personally until his death, subject, however, to the discretionary powers of expropriation by the Group Areas Development Board.[1]

The wide range and varied nature of the controls gives considerable flexibility. The powers provided in the first four types of proclaimed area listed above are means towards the ultimate goal, that of Group Areas reserved for the ownership and/or occupation of distinct racial groups. The tempo of change may thus be sharply accelerated or gradual, dependent on the length of the period during which the intermediate types of control are applied. The different gradations in control over ownership and occupation permit adjustment to the racial distribution and aspirations in each town, while flexibility is further increased by the power vested in the Minister of the Interior to issue permits relaxing the controls in individual cases.

However, notwithstanding these varied and flexible controls, the conversion of an existing pattern of racial distribution into fully segregated Group Areas may be seriously impeded by two factors: the reluctance of racially disqualified persons to move out of the areas in which they are living; and the reluctance of racially qualified persons to move into the areas designated for them. The inevitable resistance to compulsory removal from established homes can

---

[1] Our exposition of the different forms of control is based on the brief résumé by the Technical Sub-Committee on Race Zoning (Part II of the report), and on the pamphlet by K. Kirkwood, *The Group Areas Act*, previously cited (both issued prior to the amending legislation), as well as on the original statute as amended.

be reduced, in the case of property owners, by an adequate system of compensation, and, conversely, the distaste for a particular area may be modified by enhancing its residential amenities. To provide incentives for movement out of, and into, Group Areas, powers of compensation and development are conferred on the Group Areas Development Board.

When the provisions of the Group Areas Development Act are applied to an area, the procedure is that the Development Board prepares a list of 'affected' properties (that is to say, properties in the ownership or occupation of racially disqualified persons) and ensures that a 'basic value'[1] is placed on each property by a valuator or valuators appointed by the Administrator of the Province.[2] If the affected property is sold at a price above the 'basic value', the Development Board shares the excess equally with the owner. If the price is less than the 'basic value', the Board pays to the owner 80 per cent of the deficiency. The Board, that is to say, stands to gain the largest profit when the 'basic value' is well below the market price, and is exposed to the maximum danger of loss when the 'basic value' approximates to the market price. From the point of view of the owner, the provision of some compensation against loss is an inducement to sell, more particularly as it is backed by powers of expropriation; the higher the 'basic value', the greater the inducement.

[1] The 'basic value' of land is its market value immediately prior to the proclamation of the area, and in determining this value, municipal and building society valuations, and the use made of the land, must be taken into consideration. In respect of buildings, the same considerations apply, the 'basic value', however, being the cost of erection at time of valuation, less depreciation due to wear and tear, and depreciation due to the unsuitability of the building for its original or present usage, whichever is the greater. The Natal Indian Organization, in a Memorandum to the Minister of the Interior, expressed the fears of the Indian community that the 'basic value' would fall far below the true value of the property in the open market, and that the effect would be to enrich the Group Area Board at the expense of Indian property holders.

[2] An amendment is now proposed in terms of which the Board will act through its own panel of valuers, instead of through an independent valuator appointed by the Administrator.

The Board's development rights include the first option to acquire 'affected properties'[1] as well as the power to expropriate *any* immovable property in a Group Area, if it is expedient for proper development. The Board may, with Ministerial approval, develop property so acquired, build houses, and provide traditional municipal services and amenities. An area may thus be developed to attract affected persons from other areas (as, for example, by the provision of better roads and lighting in Indian areas, which are to be reserved for Europeans); or its character may be transformed (e.g. by the conversion of Mosques or Hindu Temples to Community Centres, the reconstruction of Indian homes to conform more closely to European needs, the conversion of semi-detached African homes into detached European homes). Handsome profits can be made or disastrous losses incurred in the control and manipulation of property values, while the process of Group Areas conversion may be hastened or retarded, dependent on the exercise of its powers by the Board, or by Municipalities under delegated authority from the Board.

The conversion of the present pattern of residential settlement into racially exclusive Group Areas involves the control of ecological process. The following situations may arise:

(1) A relatively homogeneous area is to be reserved for the racial group at present in possession:

(2) An area of mixed racial composition is to be reserved for a single racial group:

(3) A relatively homogeneous area in the possession of one racial group is to be reserved for another, that is to say, there is to be a complete racial metamorphosis.

Each of the three situations was carefully analysed by the Durban City Council through its Technical Sub-Committee

[1] In cases where the Board exercises the option, if the price exceeds the 'basic value', the amount payable by the Board is reduced by half this excess; if the price is less than the 'basic value', the Board pays the 'basic value' reduced by 20 per cent of the deficiency.

on Race Zoning, which submitted recommendations for controlled ecological change.[1] Using these as a basis, we may indicate briefly some of the possibilities.

The first situation, the reservation of an area for the predominant racial group, presents little difficulty. The procedure is to consolidate the *de facto* position, by proclaiming a Group Area for the Ownership and Occupation of the racial group already substantially in possession. The few racially disqualified residents would be obliged to leave the area by a specified date, unless they secured permits, while disqualified owners could continue in ownership during their life-time. The Development Board might facilitate the process of conversion by offering displaced persons attractive sites in other areas and by the exercise of its powers of acquisition.

Where racially mixed areas are to be reserved for one of the racial groups living there, the approach recommended by the Technical Sub-Committee is that of 'making the mixture leaner'. Control over occupation is used as the spearhead of change, and the technique is to proclaim a Proposed Group Area for Occupation without specifying the date on which it is to be effective. The permit system would be used simultaneously to encourage the acquisition of ownership and occupation by members of the qualified race.[2] When there is a gradual predominance of ownership and occupation by the qualified race in any section of the area, or in the area as a whole, it is proclaimed a Group Area for both Ownership and Occupation, and members of the 'wrong' race must then move out by the specified date.

The major difficulty arises in the third situation, the racial metamorphosis of an area. It is like a game of Chinese

---

[1] *Report of Technical Sub-Committee on Race Zoning*, Part II, Chapters VIII and IX. The Technical Sub-Committee made its analysis prior to the amendments of the Group Areas Act, though it envisaged the power to proclaim Proposed Group Areas for Occupation and the establishment of a Development Board.

[2] Where ownership is already held, for the most part, by members of the qualified group, but occupation is racially mixed, then the solution is to proclaim a 'Group Area for Ownership *and* Proposed Area for Occupation'.

Checkers, in which segregated clusters of white and coloured balls must change positions.[1] Clearly, unless this process is carefully controlled, there may be a stage when the white and coloured balls are almost inextricably jumbled together, that is, a stage when segregation completely breaks down. Since, in theory, the whole purpose is to maintain and perfect segregation, though in different positions, an intervening stage of intermingling is clearly intolerable. The change-over must be in compact groups of one colour.

Complicating the matter further is the fact that the racial groups cannot be handled as if they were white and coloured balls: their attitudes must be taken into account. Thus, the Technical Sub-Committee was convinced that Europeans were less tolerant than Indians of residential intermingling. Hence, it concluded that the process of converting a European to an Indian area should be relatively abrupt, as Europeans would deeply resent 'being subjected to having Indian occupied houses in between European ones'.[2] In the reverse case, since Indians have less or no repugnance for European neighbours, and since the Europeans would be entering voluntarily, a more gradual process of change-over might be tolerable, with some measure of residential intermingling. Even in the latter case, however, the Technical Sub-Committee felt that it could not recommend a process of very long-term race mixture in an area where there is little or none to begin with, since the object of the Group Areas Act is to create racial homogeneity.

The technique suggested by the City Council for racial transformation is precisely the same as for racially mixed areas, the proclamation of a Proposed Group Area for Occupation combined with the use of the permit system to

---

[1] Theoretically, whites may be moved into non-white areas, and non-whites into white areas. In practice, it is only in exceptional circumstances that non-whites are likely to move into white areas, and indeed the whole problem is much simplified by the possibility of removing non-whites to undeveloped land outside the city boundaries (i.e. to return to our analogy, the coloured balls may be moved right off the board).

[2] Ibid., p. 94.

facilitate transfer of ownership and occupation to members
of the qualified group. This is a flexible approach, and
leaves room for experiment. The procedure recommended by
the Technical Sub-Committee was more complex, a subtle
combination of control over ownership and occupation so
as to reproduce the marginal invasions and successions of
classical ecological theory, in an ordered way and with the
minimum of racial intermingling in the process. Where the
conversion of an area is from Indian to European, the role
of the Development Board will be crucial, because many
Europeans would be unwilling to buy Indian homes except
at bargain prices. By providing equitable compensation and
by enhancing the amenities of the area, the Board may
encourage Indian evacuation and attract European invasion.
The reverse case, the conversion of European to Indian
areas, is largely a theoretical possibility only, and presents
less difficulty, since European property will attract Indian
purchasers.

By employing techniques of this type, a plausible case
may be made that the compulsory segregation of the Group
Areas Act is not compulsory at all. The Durban City
Council argues along these lines, that the compulsion of the
full Group Area for Ownership and Occupation will only
be applied in racially homogeneous areas, which are to be
reserved for the race group in occupation. Small numbers
of disqualified persons would be obliged to move, but these
would normally be residents with sufficient means to acquire
or build other homes. Properties are continually changing
hands in the ordinary course of living, and the proclamation
of a full Group Area will merely channel a natural and
voluntary process in a particular direction. For the rest,
major changes will be initiated by the permissive procedures
of the proposed Group Areas for Occupation. No one will
be compelled to move: members of the 'wrong' race group
will evacuate voluntarily. Indeed, some of the movement
will be virtually slum clearance, or the attraction of better

housing, and residents as a whole will benefit by release from insecurity about the future.

The counter-argument is that the proclamation of full Group Areas deprives the disqualified group of legally acquired rights, often of long standing. There is a basic principle involved, irrespective of the numbers affected. Moreover, if compulsion is applied primarily to the members of one racial group, then again it is irrelevant that only small numbers are affected. The community as a whole suffers from discrimination and the displaced persons become symbols of racial injustice. In regard to the so-called permissive procedures of Proposed Group Areas, disqualified residents will in fact be *obliged* to move when a full Group Area is finally proclaimed. During the intervening period they will have no incentive to maintain their homes in good condition, capital will not flow into the area, and properties will deteriorate. There is such a vast shortage of houses for Non-Whites that the City Council cannot hope to cope with the additional demand arising as a result of displacement under Group Areas, and the displaced residents will have nowhere to go. The present insecurity of uncertainty is preferable to the insecurity of certainty: and, in fact, there cannot be certainty under the Group Areas Act, which is in itself an instrument for sweeping aside long-established rights.

Little purpose would be served in developing these arguments and counter-arguments, which were fully presented at the Durban sessions of the Group Areas Board. There can be little doubt that even the Proposed Group Areas for Occupation rest squarely on compulsion. This was clearly perceived by the Technical Sub-Committee which suggested that compulsion might be necessary to accelerate the change-over because of undesirable social conditions, and added that '*the sheer fact that machinery exists for enforcing change in cases where the more flexible method fails should however act as a powerful deterrent against obstructionism*'.[1]

[1] Ibid., p. 93.

The condition under which residents have the right to evacuate themselves freely is that they avail themselves of the right; it is in fact a right which consists only in obligation. The line between 'right' and 'duty', between 'voluntary evacuation' and 'compulsory removal', is not clearly defined. The position is analogous to the situation in the Old Borough prior to the 'Penetration' Commissions, where Indians were free to buy unrestricted properties anywhere they pleased, provided they segregated their purchases in the less desirable areas.

Nevertheless, there is some substance to the argument that 'natural' ecological process can be guided towards a planned segregated pattern, thus reducing the extent of compulsion. In fact, the argument may be phrased more positively—that a measure of voluntary co-operation is necessary to implement the Group Areas proposals in Durban. This becomes clear when we examine the conditions under which the movement of racial groups will be secured.

The only condition under which Europeans will co-operate is that movement and compulsion are kept to the absolute minimum. The Group Areas legislation was passed by them, and presumably, therefore, for their benefit. They would obviously mobilize effective political action, and obstruct the working of the Act, in the event of any substantial interference with their valued property rights and established homes. Moreover, that a European should be compelled by law to give up a good home in order to make way for a Non-European runs so counter to the whole structure of South African society that it could obviously be contemplated only in the most exceptional circumstances. The minimum condition for acceptance by Europeans is that they should be left, for the most part, in undisturbed occupation; such movement as does take place must be mainly from sub-standard to good housing, from poor areas to relatively desirable areas.

This very condition inevitably militates against the acceptance of the proposals by Indians, since, with the present ecological distribution, they must bear a heavy burden of movement in the interests of a compulsory segregation which is repugnant to them. What secures European co-operation guarantees Indian obstruction.

However, the Council has two major stimuli at its disposal to induce Indian movement by means short of compulsion— it can relieve the intolerable tension, and it can offer some material inducement. The Council is well aware of the extent of insecurity at the present time and has urged on the Government the need for an early proclamation of Group Areas. For over a decade now, a young and rapidly growing Indian population has been 'pegged' under conditions of great overcrowding. Rents are high and often include payment of key-money or goodwill; property values are inflated and development retarded in many areas by uncertainty as to the future. In these circumstances the pressure is such that if land is opened to Indians under security of tenure they must flow into it. More particularly the propertied classes, who feel most keenly the lack of facilities for desirable homes, will respond to the inducement of attractive building sites. But this will only reduce the pressure to a more tolerable level, without effecting a major movement of population.

The broad mass of impoverished Indian families, however, cannot afford to re-establish themselves in new areas. They have little to lose; if their shacks are pulled down they will try to build them again, and no City Council could tolerate for any length of time the forcible removal of families. The necessary stimulus for a large-scale movement of the depressed classes is the material advantage of improved housing conditions. If these are provided, it is possible that displacement will not be deeply resented, though attachment to Temples and Mosques, and ties to the community, will act as anchors. So, too, in the case of the African population, the main issue will be the rehousing of thousands of families living in shacks. The small Coloured Community is relatively favoured under the Group Areas proposals and their regrouping presents less difficulty, but even for the Coloureds provision of housing will be necessary.

It is clear then that the successful carrying out of the Group Areas plans will call for a large re-housing programme, and the benefits from compulsory segregation may not seem to the European ratepayer an adequate compensation for the very heavy costs. In any event, the crux of the matter is that displaced persons must be attracted to their new areas. There is a voluntary element in the compulsory segregation of the Group Areas, just as there was a compulsory element in the 'voluntary' segregation of the pre-war years. The theoretical distinction between the pure and the applied segregation, between the 'natural' and the 'artificial' segregation, is misleading when applied to the concrete situation in Durban.

CHAPTER VII

GROUP AREAS

THE full implications, for Town Planning, of the
Government's policy of racial separation are being
worked out in practice. Complete residential segregation is certainly a cardinal principle, and probably also
segregation of commercial, industrial and community
facilities, where possible.[1] Concentric patterns, in which
non-white residential areas 'encircle' white areas, will be
rejected, and the probability is that non-white settlement
will tend to be peripheral. Open lines of communication
are to be maintained between white areas of adjoining towns,
and non-white areas will be sited, where possible, at some
distance from main arterial routes. No model has yet been
evolved, and there will obviously be a need for a variety of
models to cover the range of urban types.

Under these conditions of exploratory racial zoning,
the pressures which the interested parties can exert at
Government and Municipal level will have a decisive
influence on the Group Areas plans for any town. Even
if the general principles were more firmly established, their
application to given conditions would still leave room

---

[1] The Durban City Council was opposed to the racial segregation of commercial and industrial facilities, and proposed the establishment of Unzoned
Working Areas. While there is no specific provision for these in the Group
Areas Act, there is also no obligation to zone the whole city. The Group
Areas Board is required to consider the desirability of establishing Group Areas
in any locality and may presumably conclude that it is undesirable, thus
leaving the locality unzoned. Nevertheless, the Government has called on
the Durban City Council to submit plans for the racial zoning of its working
areas.

for political action. The analysis of Group Areas proposals must therefore start with the groups involved, and the power which they can exert to promote their interests and policies.

The over-riding power rests with the Government. Previous South African Governments had withstood European demands for compulsory segregation.[1] The acceptance of these demands by the present Government as policy under the Group Areas Act, and the wide powers conferred for the setting aside of established rights, were therefore interpreted by sections of the European electorate as an encouragement to remove non-whites from the more desirable sections of the town, or indeed from the town itself, and, in some areas, as licence to eliminate trade competitors. As a result, the Government faces the choice, in a number of towns, between accepting plans which are extreme in their consequences for Non-Europeans, or of rejecting the plans and antagonizing the electorate.

The Government works through the Group Areas Board, whose members are appointed by the Minister of the Interior. Before the Board holds public hearings for the investigation of Group Areas in any locality, it gives notice to the public, and receives written representations. The State, the local authority under whose jurisdiction the area falls, and persons who have made applications to which the inquiry relates, are entitled to appear and be represented at the hearings, as of right; other bodies and persons may participate at the discretion of the Board. The procedures at the hearings allow for the summoning of witnesses and their interrogation under oath, and argument is presented

[1] The Government report, which preceded the Group Areas legislation, emphasized that one Government after another had failed to accede to the demands by both the English- and Afrikaans-speaking sections of the white population for the compulsory segregation of Asiatics (*Report of the Asiatic Land Tenure Laws Amendments Committee and the Land Tenure Act Amendments Committee*, previously cited, p. 9).

as in Courts of Law. Initially, a Planning and Reference Committee, also Government-appointed, assisted the Board by negotiating with local authorities, co-ordinating plans, and making recommendations.

The Group Areas Board is, however, not a Court of Law, but an administrative committee whose task it is to advise the Minister on the establishment of Group Areas. There are no general principles of law from which the Board can derive its specific recommendations for the racial zoning of areas. The only requirement under the Group Areas Act is that the Board *take into consideration* whether or not suitable accommodation will be available for persons displaced from Group Areas for Occupation or Ownership, and, as we have seen, no obligation is laid on the Board to act on any such consideration, or *to ensure* that accommodation *is* in fact available. The application of general principles of equity, as, for example, that there should be equality of sacrifice between the races, is unrealistic when one of the racial groups has the monopoly of political power; and the function of the Board is to interpret the Government policy of racial separation in the context of the forces operating in a given situation. Where, however, there is already a clearly defined pattern of segregation in a town, acceptable to the Council, the problem may be merely that of rationalizing the *status quo*.

The proposals of the local authority, as the body responsible for the administration of the area in its jurisdiction, must inevitably carry weight with the Group Areas Board. The hearings of the Group Areas Board and the deliberations of the local authorities are thus the main points at which effective pressure can be exerted by the racial groups for the promotion of their interests, though representations can also be made direct to the Government.

The local authority may refuse to submit proposals or act reluctantly under pressure from the Government, or—and

M

this is the more usual case—it may co-operate in plans for racial zoning and compulsory segregation. Where, as in Durban, the councillors are all European, and the electorate almost entirely so, and where, moreover, there is a history of racial conflict over land and property, the City Council cannot fail to become an instrument for expressing the interests of Europeans. Nevertheless, a City Council, however constituted, has certain obligations to all racial groups and, in the attempt to discharge these obligations, may submit a plan which is contrary to the interests of a section of the European population. Pressure is then brought to bear directly on the city councillors for the area affected, with a high prospect of success, since the pressure is backed by the threat of rejection at the next municipal election. If a number of areas are affected, then the needed reciprocity between city councillors would ensure a substantial bloc urging revision of the plans. If only one area is affected, as, for example, by the proposal to establish an Indian Group Area near by, then the councillors may be divided, each section frantically hitting the Indian shuttlecock out of its own area.[1]

Alternatively, or in addition, pressure may be exercised indirectly by stirring up public opinion against the City Council's proposals. The City Council is then placed in the intolerable position of subordinating European interests to Non-European, and a purely local issue is thus transformed into a wider problem of race relations. It is difficult for City Councils to resist this pressure and, if they did, the aggrieved Europeans would still have the right to make representations to the Group Areas Board; or they might approach the Government direct on the assumption that, as

---

[1] This was the situation in the capital, Pretoria. Similarly, in Durban there were signs of animosity between different groups of European residents, when the Technical Sub-Committee proposed the reservation of the interfluve area for Indians, while reserving Durban North for Europeans. Some residents in the southern districts argued that the people of Durban North could better afford to give up their homes.

the protagonist of the white group, it would not subordinate European interests.[1]

Since European interests are most effectively promoted through ratepayers' associations exerting pressure on the City Council, the role of political parties is a minor one. Only the Nationalist (Government) Party in Durban submitted proposals direct to the Group Areas Board. These proposals were opposed by the Durban City Council, on the grounds that the effect would be to reserve most of the city for Europeans; that about 130,000 Indians, almost the entire population, would be compelled to move into undeveloped land, and that no provision was made for the African population.[2] The animus shown against the Indians reflects the Nationalist Party attitude towards them as alien and unassimilable, and also the rivalry of the Afrikaner group in Durban, striving for more desirable dwelling areas.

In theory, Non-Europeans have the same possibilities of action as Europeans, that is representations to the City Council, the Group Areas Board and the Government, made either by ratepayers' associations or by non-parliamentary

[1] The Durban North Ratepayers Association, for example, in an attempt to remove the Indians from their long-established settlement north of the Umgeni River, brought pressure to bear on the city councillors for the area, and made representations both to the City Council and the Group Areas Board. Or again, European residents in Sherwood made representations direct to the Group Areas Board and the Minister of the Interior, when the Durban City Council refused their demand for the demolition of houses which were being built as an extension of the Sparks Coloured Housing Scheme. They objected to this extension because a few Coloured homes would be in full view of their own, and rejected the Council's offer of other accommodation as well as the alternative suggestion of a buffer strip of trees and shrubs (*Natal Mercury*, 3rd May 1955).

[2] See the City Council's comments on these proposals, pages 8–9 of its *Memorandum on Group Area Proposals published by Land Tenure Advisory Board*, dated 19th February 1953. The Race Zoning Commission of the Durban Branch of the Nationalist Party recommended that the greatest part of the sea coast, to a distance of three miles inland, should be in white hands. Heavy industry in Durban should be discouraged, as a precaution against war from the East, and all important roads, railway lines and water pipes should be situated in European areas. On the other hand, the Commission asserted the principle that provision of alternative housing must precede removal.

political organizations. However, since they lack the crucial argument of an effective vote,[1] the practical choice for Non-Europeans is between co-operation in the hope of securing some concessions, and non-co-operation, either in an attempt to defeat the plans, or as a matter of principle. These alternatives are embodied in the rival policies of the Natal Indian Organization and the Natal Indian Congress.

Both organizations are agreed on the rejection of compulsory segregation. The Natal Indian Organization argues, however, that compulsory segregation will be imposed in any event, and it therefore advocates the submission of alternate proposals, in an attempt to alleviate the hardships and sacrifices. This generally involves the acceptance of many aspects of the plans prepared by City Councils, which may use the area of common agreement as a springboard for its further demands, and not as a basis for negotiation and compromise.[2] Moreover, the submission of alternate plans raises the difficulty of determining what sections of the population are to be sacrificed. Any proposal by an Indian organization for the allocation to Indians of an area in which even a small number of Africans and Coloureds live can only inflame the racial antagonism of other Non-Europeans against the Indians. Even if there are no Coloureds or Africans living in the area, the consequences may still be detrimental to race relations, since, on the initiative of the Indian group, Coloureds and Africans would be deprived of the right to acquire ownership or occupation in the area. Within the Indian group there still remains the problem of unequal sacrifice, and the Natal Indian Congress alleges that the Natal Indian Organization, as representative of the merchant group,

---

[1] In September 1952 the Parliamentary roll for Durban had 76,827 White voters and 449 Coloured; the municipal electorate for 1951/2 consisted of 56,679 White and Coloured voters, and 22 Indian voters.

[2] The representatives of the City Council of Durban did precisely this at the Group Areas hearings.

seeks to promote its own commercial interests at the expense of the broad mass of the Indian people. The Natal Indian Organization, on the contrary, claims that its policy serves the Indian people better than the intransigent attitude of the Congress.

Congress rejects the basic assumption made by the Government that harmonious race relations depend on the avoidance of contact, and denies that racial harmony is in fact the purpose of the plans submitted under the Group Areas Act. It sees the true aim as the redistribution of wealth and resources in favour of the Europeans, and the removal of Non-Europeans from their developed areas of residence and trade to the remote outskirts of the towns and cities, far from the centres of commerce and industry. The main target of the Group Areas Act, according to Congress, is the Indian population, so as to encourage expatriation by making continued living in South Africa intolerable,[1] and Congress has not hesitated to describe some of the proposed plans as 'legalized robbery'. It cites, as evidence that the Group Areas Act will create racial disharmony, the manifest injustice arising from inequality of sacrifice, and the destruction of settled Non-European communities with complete disregard for the sentimental, cultural and economic ties, and the religious, educational and other community institutions, built up over the generations.

[1] Congress draws attention to the following comment by the Government-appointed committee, whose recommendations were substantially embodied in the Group Areas Act:

'The fundamental theme of the evidence throughout the years has been and still is: repatriation or, failing which, compulsory segregation. In the most recent evidence there is noticeable a distinct tendency for this theme to assume the form of repatriation and, pending which, compulsory segregation. In its most advanced form this theme reads: repatriation and, failing which, compulsory segregation with boycott to induce repatriation. The recommendations which we propose to make are such that legislation based on them would, on the one hand, not unduly endanger the possibility of repatriation, and, on the other hand, not fall short of what we regard as necessary to deal effectively with the present situation.' (*Joint Report of the Asiatic Land Tenure Laws Amendment Committee and the Land Tenure Acts Amendment Committee*, U.G. 49/1950, p. 10.)

Congress diverges from the Natal Indian Organization, not so much in its assumptions about the objectives of the Group Areas Act as in its conclusions. In the view of Congress, the submission of alternate proposals is not justified on grounds of expediency, since it has failed to secure concessions, and it is wrong in principle, since it is an acquiescence in the injustices of the Group Areas Act, though given under duress. At the Group Areas hearings in Durban, the representatives of both the Congress and the Organization directed their examinations to establish that the City Council had applied its race-zoning standards consistently for the benefit of Europeans at the expense of Non-Europeans, and drew attention to the grave consequences of the proposals. When it appeared, during the course of cross-examination, that an area occupied by Europeans might be claimed for Indians with some justice, if the City Council's criteria were applied impartially, the Organization explicitly rejected this claim, since, in common with Congress, it was opposed to the dissolution of communities of any race. The main differences between them were that the Organization sought to secure the acceptance of the principle that Group Areas proposals should not disturb settled Indian communities, and behaved in a conciliatory way, whereas Congress reacted to the Group Areas Board and to the City Council as enemies of the Non-European peoples, and consistently repudiated the whole concept of Group Areas.

This repudiation of Group Areas was expressed also by the African National Congress, Natal, 'as the only national organization of the African people in Natal,' in a memorandum to the Group Areas Board. The memorandum alleges that the sole purpose of the Group Areas Act, in relation to the African peoples, is to deprive them of the free occupation and ownership of land, so as to ensure that they will be Government tenants at all times, and hence a source of cheap labour. The City Council is charged with such neglect of its African citizens, due to the fact that they do not enjoy any franchise rights, that an estimated 80,000 live in shacks, under wretched and disgraceful conditions. The plans, according to Congress, would have the effect of uprooting the entire African population from the Borough of Durban, and depriving them, in the process, of their present municipal locations and of even the meagre 105 acres they now own. The dominating feature of the proposed racial zoning of Durban was found in the callous disregard of the needs and aspirations of the African people.[1]

This was not a complaint that could be made by the Coloureds against the City Council's proposals, since they were the most favoured of the Non-European groups, though even the Coloureds faced a large-scale resettlement. Their objections, at the Group Areas hearings in Durban, related to the whole principle of compulsory segregation, which they attacked as contrary to the Brotherhood of Man and the Fatherhood of God, and as an ill-conceived attempt to promote racial harmony. They were opposed to confinement in segregated areas for the rest of their days, and pointed out that many Coloureds had passed into the European group. It is impossible to say to what extent these views were representative. Exercising the municipal vote, though in small numbers, they have other channels for making their reactions known. They are a divided community, and some sections in fact favour racial zoning, as a means of preserving their more privileged position in relation to other Non-European groups.

These, then, were the attitudes of the organized racial groups in Durban, and the pressures they could exert on the

[1] There are divergent interests within the African population. African traders have some interest in racial zoning and the elimination from their Group Areas of India trade competitors, and some are beginning to work towards this end. The position of the Indian trader is parlous, threatened as he is by emerging Afrikaans and African trading classes, both with advantages to gain by the application of the Group Areas Act against the Indian population.

planning of Group Areas. The result of this play of forces can be analysed readily by comparing the first plans prepared by the Technical Sub-Committee of the City Council in November 1951, with the final plans adopted by the City Council in August 1952.

The Technical Sub-Committee, consisting of senior municipal officials, approached its task of Group Areas planning in the spirit of technical experts and not as politicians. Nevertheless, its freedom to plan was severely limited by political compulsions, both national and local.

The over-riding political compulsion arose from the nature of the task itself, the framing of proposals for compulsory racial segregation under the Group Areas Act. The Sub-Committee, acting apparently from conviction rather than compulsion, laid strong emphasis on the avoidance of inter-racial contact, and indeed extended the principle well beyond the legal requirements. Power to proclaim Border Strips, in the absence of natural or other barriers between Group Areas, was only conferred on the Governor-General in 1955, and the Group Areas Act to this day does not prohibit the passage of members of one racial group through the residential area of another.

The insistence by the Sub-Committee on effective, preferably natural, barriers between residential areas, and on direct access to place of work, imposed the main outlines of a radial plan, based on the river systems of Durban. Nature had certainly been accommodating enough to provide four rivers spreading fan-wise from the business areas, but without any prevision of the racial composition of Durban in 1951: the populations of European, Indian and African are almost equal, the space between the rivers quite unequal. Moreover, the existing pattern of racial settlement is partly concentric and partly radial, more particularly in the south and along the river banks and main arterial roads.[1] Inevitably then, the Sub-Committee's selection of criteria imposed on it the dilemma of choosing between the mass movement of peoples for the sake of a radial river-based plan, or compromise on its plan to preserve established settlements. The dilemma was, however, only partly self-imposed; the Sub-Committee would still have been under the political compulsion to plan for racial segregation, even if it had concluded, on a more detailed examination of the problem, that racial contact promotes harmony.

The second major compulsion was the determination of the Minister of Native Affairs that Cato Manor should be converted to European use. This large tract of land, about one-tenth of the total area of Durban, lying in the peripheral zone of the Added Areas, and cut off from the cooling sea-breeze by the Central Berea Ridge to the east, is not desired by Europeans. Ecologically, it is the area in which we would have expected an impoverished Non-European population to settle, and it is, in fact, almost entirely Non-European in character, housing some 11,381 Indians, 27,652 Africans, and 1,040 Coloureds, but only 21 Europeans.[2] One of the main Non-European settled areas of Durban, Cato Manor includes an Indian housing scheme, large slum African shack

[1] The concentric pattern is most clearly marked in the Old Borough. Moving westward in the central areas between the Umbilo and Umgeni Rivers, we have a band of European settlement on the sea front, followed by Non-European settlements on the alluvial flats and the lower slopes of the central ridge. Then comes a band of European settlement, with incomes rising towards the boundaries of the Old Borough on the crest of the ridge. West of the Old Borough boundaries is the large expanse of predominantly poor Non-European settlement in Cato Manor, and, beyond the present city boundaries, the wealthy European homes in the dormitory town of Westville.
The South constitutes a distinctive sector. It is predominantly Non-European in residential character and not specially attractive for European residents. In the North there are the two main bands—of European settlement on the ridge and of Non-European inland, with Indian residents, however, settled along the banks of the Umgeni River.
[2] According to the estimate of the Technical Sub-Committee (*Factual Report on Alternative Race Zoning Proposals*, dated 24th March 1952, Table No. 1). Cato Manor falls in Census Tracts 23 and 24, which have a population of 19,357 Indians, 36,222 Africans, 1,504 Coloureds and 1,134 Europeans.

settlements, a modern African location, and an estate set
aside for African freehold ownership. There is considerable
Indian investment in homes, shops, land and such community facilities as Government-aided Schools, vernacular
schools, Mosques, Temples, cemeteries, a modern crema-
torium and a cinema.[1] Again, the Technical Sub-Committee
appears to have become convinced, independently, of the
necessity for the removal of the Non-European population,
so as to create a broad homogeneous area of European
settlement between the Umgeni and Umbilo rivers, extending from the eastern slopes of the central ridge to the
adjoining town of Westville, and protected from Non-
European movement to place of work. And again, the
Technical Sub-Committee had no alternative but to
comply with the demands of the Minister of Native
Affairs.[2]

The final compulsion, at Government level, arises
indirectly from the Government's land policy. Native
Reserves and Native Trust Lands are excluded from the
operation of the Group Areas Act, with the result that the
two Native Reserves outside the southern and the north-
western boundaries of the city are fixed in racial character.
Since the Sub-Committee favoured large racial zones, with
room for expansion and natural increase, the site of the
African zones within the city was predetermined, namely in

[1] One of the witnesses at the hearings by the Group Areas Board stated that
there were 69 shops, 4 clothing factories, 2 box factories, 1 bicycle factory,
10 Government-aided Schools, 7 vernacular schools, 5 Temples, 2 Mosques,
5 Indian Cemeteries, and a variety of other community investments. Dr S.
Cooppan, in a paper on 'The Implications of the Group Areas Act for Indian
Education' presented to the Conference on Group Areas convened by the
Natal Indian Congress on the 5th–6th May 1956, gives the number of Government-aided Schools in 1955, in the Mayville–Cato Manor area, as 19 (8 being
'platoon' or afternoon schools), with a total enrolment of 5,608 students.

[2] The Durban City Council had already given the Minister the assurance
that Cato Manor would be reserved for Europeans (see footnote to page 145
of the Technical Sub-Committee's report). The Council did so reluctantly,
and under compulsion, because the Minister imposed it as a condition for his
consent to a temporary and urgently needed African settlement scheme in
Cato Manor, and because the Council interpreted the Minister's demand as a
statement of Government policy.

areas on the south-western and north-western perimeter of the city, adjacent to the Reserves.

At local Government level, the Sub-Committee regarded the reservation for Europeans of the Upper Berea Ridge and the Beach Front as so self-evident that it did not even advance the argument that these areas were very largely European and that the tourist and hotel industries of Durban catered for Europeans. The most desirable and valuable residential areas of the city were therefore allocated to Europeans. In the same way it must have been axiomatic that the wealthy European residential suburb of Durban North, with its fine sea views and cooling sea-breezes, would be reserved for Europeans, though in this case the Sub-Committee justified its decision on the ground that the quality of housing was far superior to that which Non-Europeans, in general, could afford to buy. The same argument could have been applied in the case of the substantial homes on the Central Berea Ridge.

Embedded in the thinking of the Sub-Committee, though not as compulsions, were certain local Government ideas. There was the vision of an Indian town outside Durban, conceived by some as a means for removing the Indians from Durban, and by the Sub-Committee as a way of providing a measure of local autonomy and room for the anticipated large increase in the Indian population. So, too, the idea of racial zoning on a regional radial pattern was not new, but already incorporated in a vision of housing accommodation 'for the future of all times', revealed to the City Valuator and Estates Manager as early as 1943.[1]

[1] *Programme of Post-War Development: Report of Special Committee* (Durban, September 1953), p. 19. The constructive idealism of the war years, expressed in plans for a brave new world, infused also the post-war development plans of the Durban City Council. The unusual feature was the emphasis on racial zoning. Many of the elements of the Sub-Committee's later plans are to be found in this report: racial zoning based on the river-systems with their natural barriers; the radial pattern, though with less disturbance of settled areas; large zones, capable of expansion; the siting of residential areas in relation to places of employment, and the establishment of a 'satellite' Indian city.

[*Footnote continued on next page.*

Freedom to plan was severely limited by the combination of the Sub-Committee's radical criteria for racial zoning, and the framework of Government and municipal restrictions within which the criteria were applied to the physiographic features of Durban. Given these fixed points of reference, most of the plan was in fact predetermined.

The Group Areas proposals by the Technical Sub-Committee are shown in Figure 21. Apart from the working zones round the Bay and on the Alluvial Flats, the entire area between the Umgeni and Umbilo Rivers, from the sea to Westville, was allocated to Europeans. Within the commercial centre of the working areas, residential occupation was reserved for Europeans in the European section, and left unzoned in the Indian section. In effect, then, the Technical Sub-Committee eliminated Indian 'penetration', and absorbed, moreover, into working zones or into European residential zones, the seven areas demarcated by the First 'Penetration' Commission[1] as predominantly Indian in 1927. Not an acre of land in the Old Borough remained as a racial zone for Indians, while in the Added Areas west of the central ridge, the major Non-European settlements of Cato Manor, Springfield, Sydenham and Clare Estate were destined for gradual conversion to European occupation.

The Sub-Committee dealt in the same way with the sea front from north to south, reserving all the residential areas for Europeans and eliminating the old Indian settlements of Riverside and Prospect Hall immediately north of the Umgeni River (tract 5). The northern ridge, stretching along the sea front from the Umgeni River to Umhlanga

Footnote continued from previous page.]

The Provincial authorities also inquired into the problems of racial zoning and prepared a regional radial plan for Durban and the surrounding districts. They emphasized, in the *Ninth Interim Report of the Post-War Works and Reconstruction Commission regarding Provincial and Town Planning* (January 1945), the avoidance of 'racial islands', and the attraction of the races to their zones in preference to forcible transplanting—concepts accepted also by the Technical Sub-Committee.   [1] See Chapter VI, pp. 149–50.

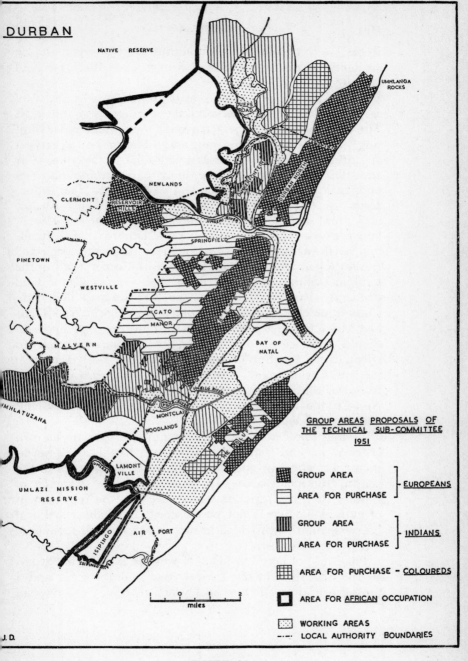

DURBAN

NATIVE RESERVE

UMHLANGA ROCKS

DUFFS ROAD

NEWLANDS

CLERMONT

RESERVOIR HILLS

UMGENI RIVER

SPRINGFIELD

PINETOWN

WESTVILLE

CATO MANOR

BAY OF NATAL

MALVERN

UMHLATUZANA

MONTCLAIR

WOODLANDS

LAMONT VILLE

THE BLUFF

UMLAZI MISSION RESERVE

AIR PORT

ISIPINGO

GROUP AREAS PROPOSALS OF THE TECHNICAL SUB-COMMITTEE 1951

▨	GROUP AREA	EUROPEANS
▭	AREA FOR PURCHASE	
▥	GROUP AREA	INDIANS
▥	AREA FOR PURCHASE	
▦	AREA FOR PURCHASE - COLOUREDS	
▢	AREA FOR AFRICAN OCCUPATION	
⣿	WORKING AREAS	
–·–	LOCAL AUTHORITY BOUNDARIES	

miles

J. D.

FIGURE 21

Rocks, well beyond the boundaries of the city, and the residential areas on the Ocean Ridge of the Bluff, were all allocated to Europeans.

For each of the Non-European groups, two zones were carefully sited on and beyond the perimeters of the city. The Coloureds were allocated a small area on the inner Bluff ridge, away from the sea-front, and a large zone to the west of Durban North. The African zones fell to the south-west and the north-west, for the most part outside the city boundaries and adjoining the Native Reserves. The Indian zones were placed between the European and African areas, and served almost as buffers—one in the north-west, between two railway lines (Duikerfontein area) and extending northwards across the boundary into the projected Indian town, and the other in the south, incorporating the Umbilo-Umhlatuzana Interfluve and a long rib of land stretching westwards beyond the city limits. The Sub-Committee left the southern section of the ridge at Woodlands and Montclair unzoned, indicating, however, that this area should be allocated to one of the non-European groups. In effect, then, the Sub-Committee proposed the reservation for Non-Europeans of most of the southern districts, apart from the Bluff, recognizing in this way the predominantly Non-European character of the south in terms of residence and employment.

Testing the Technical Sub-Committee's plan by its own criteria, we find that barriers between racial zones are at their most effective and most natural as boundaries to the central European area. In other zones, use is made of railway lines and arterial roads. Clearly, the requirement of natural barriers is not peremptory, and indeed artificial barriers could be provided in most areas, though sometimes at considerable cost.

Proximity of home to place of work is assured, in theory, by the allocation of the central zone to Europeans, and a northern and southern zone to each of the Non-European groups. The argument advanced by the Technical Sub-Committee that the central zone should be reserved for Europeans, because they are employed for the most part in that zone, could be inverted; the number of Non-Europeans employed in the central areas far exceeds the number of Europeans, and Non-Europeans can least afford to pay for transport or to run their own cars. In any event, the location of the home in relation to place of work is determined by many factors, of which proximity is only one. The shortage of houses is especially crucial in the case of Non-Europeans, many of whom, particularly in the industrially undeveloped northern areas, might well find themselves obliged to live at one end of the city while working in the other. The effect of the race-zoning proposals would be to remove some of the poorest groups farthest from the main areas of employment. On the other hand, the difficulty of the longer journey to work was mitigated by the careful siting of the Non-European areas close to cheap rail transport.

The requirement of direct access to industrial and commercial areas, without traversing the residential zones of other race groups, is met by extending the working areas in a long band from north to south. The extreme consequences of this apparently minor criterion are best illustrated in its use to support the recommendation for the redistribution of Non-Europeans in the areas west of the central ridge. The racial zones are large, allowing for expansion of the racial group within the zone, and for a measure of local autonomy in Indian and African Group Areas. But the pattern of zoning is not radial. The sea-front residential areas are reserved for Europeans, in a band stretching from north to south. Then follow the commercial and industrial areas, and it is from these that the remaining residential zones radiate. The proposals are thus a combination of concentric and radial patterns, as is the present racial distribution of the population.

In general, the Technical Sub-Committee's plan involves the redistribution of resources in favour of Europeans, the dissolution of settled communities, mainly Non-European, and the reservation of the most desirable land for exclusive European use. The net gain to Europeans, at the expense of Indians, is almost 3,000 acres within the city, which would have the effect of increasing European holdings to about 19,400 acres and reducing Indian holdings to some 7,500 acres. The value of European investments in the city, as a result of this redistribution, would rise by £6,000,000 to £120,000,000, while Indian investment would fall to about £18,500,000.[1] Indians could naturally reinvest in the new areas allotted to them, but their major losses would be in the better residential suburbs.

The main burden of movement within the city falls on the Non-Europeans—a displacement of over 70,000 Indians, some 8,500 Coloureds, and almost 40,000 Africans from the areas west of the Old Borough alone,[2] as compared with a total European displacement of less than 12,000 (excluding the southern section of the ridge at Woodlands and Montclair which was left unzoned). The extent of population redistribution would have been even greater, but for the policy of permitting residential settlement in the working zones, and its impact even more severe, but for the gradual procedures advocated in the transformation of homogeneous and mixed racial zones. The evacuation of the residentially desirable areas, the sea-front and the central ridge, accounts

[1] Based on Table V and VI, Part III, of the Technical Sub-Committee's report. The balance of profit and loss shown by the Technical Sub-Committee is £2,000,000 less than ours, since it compensated Indians with the township of Malvern, which falls outside the jurisdiction of the city of Durban.

[2] These are the main areas of unplanned African settlement. The population figures for the African population west of the Old Borough boundaries are those given by the Technical Sub-Committee (TABLE IV, REPORT ON RACE ZONING UPON ALTERNATIVE PROPOSALS PUT FORWARD BY COUNCIL-IN-COMMITTEE, dated 30th January 1952). African displacement in the remainder of the city is more difficult to calculate, since it depends on policy in regard to barracks, hostels and residence on employers' premises.

for only part of this large-scale redistribution of Non-Europeans.[1]

The Technical Sub-Committee thus imposed the main burden of movement on the Non-Europeans, but at the same time it asked for a small measure of reciprocity by suggesting the allocation to Indians of a European settlement in the south. In discussing the determinants of its plan, the Sub-Committee had assumed that it was free to move Europeans from their homes. There was high authority for this assumption, since the Minister of the Interior had declared, during the second reading of the Group Areas Bill, that 'we want justice done to the Non-European groups' (p. 7820); that 'we must find living room for the Non-Europeans, the Europeans will have to make sacrifices' (7827); and that segregation 'is achieved without recourse to discrimination between the various races. The restrictions imposed on one group are also imposed on the other groups. Each group surrenders certain of its rights for the common good of all groups' (7452).[2]

The assumption was, however, based on a misconception of the political process—that a group with an effective monopoly of political power would inflict sacrifices on itself, when the laws provide the necessary means for material advantage. Moreover, in the proposed rewriting of the ecology of Durban, the Europeans do not constitute a single group, but a number of groups, and the suggestion that some of these groups should bear the whole burden of European sacrifice naturally appeared unjust. The affected groups mobilized and speedily corrected the Sub-Committee's misconceptions.

Immediately on the release of the proposals, opposition

[1] Our estimate of the minimum movement necessary for complete segregation between Indians and Europeans in the census tracts was a movement of 14·71 per cent of Europeans and 6·25 per cent of Indians (p. 156), as compared with the Technical Sub-Committee's recommendation for the movement of less than 10 per cent Europeans and more than 50 per cent Indians. Of course, the Sub-Committee was not planning for minimum movement.

[2] Hansard, *House of Assembly Debates*, vols. 70–3, 8th May to 24th June 1950.

N

began to crystallize among the city councillors. One declared that he would 'fight to see that no developed area in Durban now occupied by Europeans should be handed to Indians', and another that he would 'never be party to the forceful taking away from Europeans of anything they own—their own homes'. The residents themselves held a series of protest meetings, offered money in the fight, and pledged themselves to a 'last ditch stand'. Reflecting the intense emotional reactions, one of the meetings opened with mass responses to questions from the public platform. 'Are you prepared to let your homes, which represent your life savings, be taken from you?' 'Are you willing in every way to fight this iniquitous proposal?' There were demands for the repatriation of Indians, and calls on Europeans to band together. The Technical Sub-Committee had forgotten 'the human element', as one city councillor phrased it.

Within two months the Council-in-Committee reintroduced the human element. It instructed the Sub-Committee to prepare new plans reserving the suburbs between the Umbilo and Umhlatuzana Rivers and the southern section of the ridge for Europeans. The natural desire of people to stay on in their homes was recognized, and the sanctity of the homestead upheld. The effect, however, was to impose on over 6,000 Indians a sacrifice which had provoked the European residents to a 'last ditch' stand in defence of their rights.

Indeed, the Council-in-Committee went farther still, and conceded almost all the demands of organized European groups, whether these demands arose from objections to dictated movement or to the presence of Non-Europeans in adjoining neighbourhoods. So extensive were the proposed concessions that the Sub-Committee was constrained to comment that the revised plan virtually confined displacement to Non-Europeans.[1] This remains the effect, too, of the final plans adopted by the City Council on the 5th August

---

[1] *Report of Technical Sub-Committee on Race Zoning upon alternative proposals put forward by Council-in-Committee*, dated 30th January 1952, p. 5.

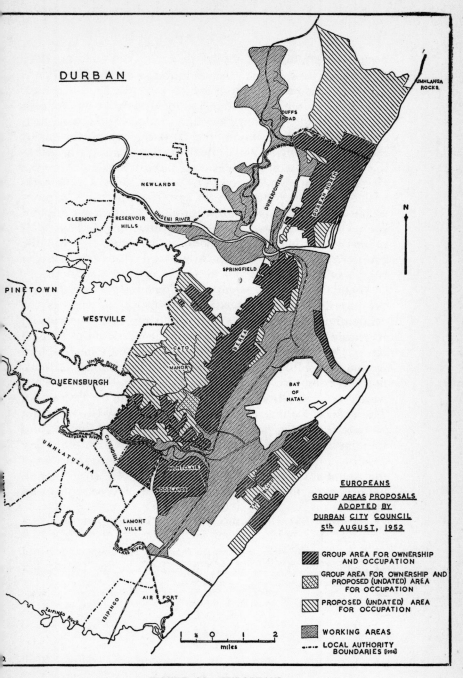

DURBAN

NEWLANDS

CLERMONT · RESERVOIR HILLS

UNGENI RIVER

SPRINGFIELD

PINETOWN

WESTVILLE

Umgeni River

CATO MANOR

BEREA

QUEENSBURGH

UMHLATUZANA

CAVENDISH

MONTCLAIR

WOODLANDS

LAMONT VILLE

UMLAAS RIVER

ISIPINGO RIVER

ISIPINGO

AIR PORT

DUFFS ROAD

DUIKERFONTEIN

DURBAN NORTH

UMHLANGA ROCKS.

BAY OF NATAL

N

EUROPEANS
GROUP AREAS PROPOSALS
ADOPTED BY
DURBAN CITY COUNCIL
5th AUGUST, 1952

GROUP AREA FOR OWNERSHIP
AND OCCUPATION

GROUP AREA FOR OWNERSHIP AND
PROPOSED (UNDATED) AREA
FOR OCCUPATION

PROPOSED (UNDATED) AREA
FOR OCCUPATION

WORKING AREAS

LOCAL AUTHORITY
BOUNDARIES [1956]

½ O 1 2
miles

FIGURE 22: EUROPEANS

1952, after a number of revisions.[1] Europeans maintain their settlements, and extend their holdings of desirable land.

Figure 22 shows the Group Areas proposals for Europeans, submitted by the City Council to the Group Areas Board in February 1953. The dark hatchings indicate areas proposed for immediate reservation, the lighter hatchings areas for more gradual conversion, while the dotted areas refer to working zones. Adjoining towns and districts are included, the city boundaries being marked by a heavy line. Comparison with Figures 21 (p. 189), 16 (p. 137) and 11 (p. 97), demonstrates the changes effected in the Sub-Committee's original proposals, the extent to which European settlement is preserved and extended, and the relationship between the proposed European Group Areas and the physiographic regions of Durban.

Almost the entire ridge, north, centre and south, and the interfluve are allocated to Europeans, as well as the residential areas on the sea front,[2] with the exception of Riverside (portion of tract 5 immediately north of the Umgeni River), which is left unzoned, and the extreme southern section of the Bluff, which is proposed for Indians. In the north the wealthy European settlements are extended westwards so as to eliminate the suggested zone for Coloureds. The central European section still reaches to Westville but is now extended southwards beyond the Umbilo and Umhlatuzana Rivers to include Woodlands and Montclair (tract 34 on the southern section of the ridge) and portion of the Stainbank Estate (originally proposed for Indians, and lying outside the city boundaries, west of Woodlands and

---

[1] *The Durban Housing Survey*, op. cit., Chapter XV, gives a précis of these plans, of the Technical Sub-Committee's main report, and of earlier proposals for racial zoning.

[2] The reservation of the northern sea front area for Europeans is carried along the coast line to Umhlanga Rocks well beyond the city boundaries. When it was suggested at the hearings of the Group Areas Board that Indians might be given access to the sea on the coast line south of Umhlanga Rocks, the City Council's representative objected that the Europeans at Umhlanga Rocks would be '*cut off*' from Durban (*Natal Daily News*, 10th August 1953).

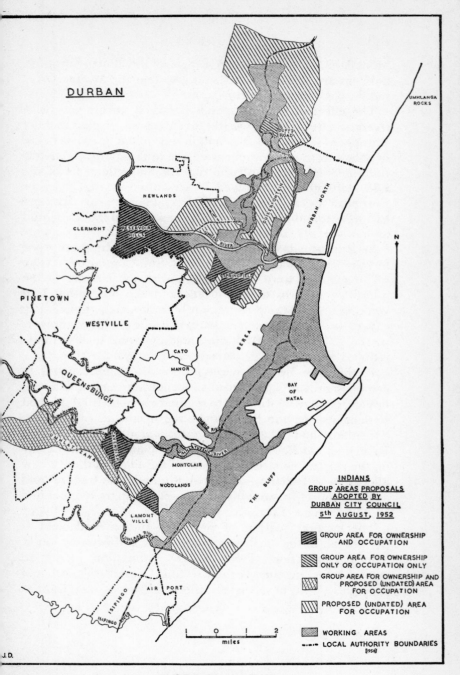

DURBAN

NEWLANDS

CLERMONT

RESERVOIR HILLS

SPRINGFIELD

PINETOWN

WESTVILLE

CATO MANOR

QUEENSBURGH

BEREA

UMHLATUZANA

MONTCLAIR

WOODLANDS

LAMONT VILLE

ISIPINGO

AIR PORT

UMHLANGA ROCKS

DUFFS ROAD

DURBAN NORTH

UMGENI RIVER

BAY OF NATAL

THE BLUFF

UMLAZI RIVER

UMHLATUZANA RIVER

UMBILO RIVER

N

INDIANS
GROUP AREAS PROPOSALS
ADOPTED BY
DURBAN CITY COUNCIL
5th AUGUST, 1952

GROUP AREA FOR OWNERSHIP
AND OCCUPATION

GROUP AREA FOR OWNERSHIP
ONLY OR OCCUPATION ONLY

GROUP AREA FOR OWNERSHIP AND
PROPOSED (UNDATED) AREA
FOR OCCUPATION

PROPOSED (UNDATED) AREA
FOR OCCUPATION

WORKING AREAS

---- LOCAL AUTHORITY BOUNDARIES
[1958]

1 0 1 2
miles

J. D.

FIGURE 23: INDIANS

Montclair). On the Ocean Ridge of the Bluff, European holdings are carried farther south, so that the Marine Drive should pass through European areas.

The effect of these proposals is largely to dispense with rivers as natural boundaries between zones. Displacement of Europeans is reduced to a minimum, about 3,100 persons, over half from a Government village in the south. 'Penetration' is eliminated, and the old Indian settlements of the Old Borough are dissolved either into working zones or European areas. The main residential core of the city from east to west and north to south, indeed most of the residential area of the city, is reserved for Europeans.

Serious inroads were thus made into the holdings proposed for the Indians by the Technical Sub-Committee. The major changes were in the south, with the transfer of the interfluve suburbs to Europeans and the absorption into working zones of the predominantly Indian area immediately east of the interfluve; (compare Figure 23 with Figure 21, p. 189). The proposed Indian holdings were thus virtually reduced to land outside the city boundaries.

It therefore became necessary for the City Council to compensate Indians. This compensation took the form, largely, of allowing Indians to retain some of their established settlements—on the Bluff in the south, and at Springfield, Sydenham and Clare Estate (south-west of the Umgeni River), and at Newlands (north of the Umgeni River). Only on the extreme western perimeter of the city was there a new allocation to Indians—a residentially desirable tract of land at Reservoir Hills, not fully developed and sparsely inhabited by some twenty European families.

The general pattern of proposed Indian settlement is peripheral, in the north-west, south-west and extreme south. The redistribution of the Indian population is not so extensive as in the Technical Sub-Committee's original proposals,[1] but nevertheless affects about 55,000 Indians

[1] Compare Figures 23 (p. 197), 21 (p. 189), and 18 (p. 140).

within the city.[1] Of the 18 census tracts in which 94 per cent of the Indian population live (Table XXXV, p. 155), 2 are proposed entirely, and 5 partly, for Indians, while the remaining 11 tracts are absorbed into European areas, a Coloured area and working zones.

The extent of land holdings for Europeans and Indians within the city remains substantially as in the Sub-Committee's original plan, with this important difference, however, that a smaller acreage of *developed* land now accrues to Indians.[2] The effect is to destroy the Sub-Committee's carefully devised procedures for starting the process of population exchange by attracting displaced persons to developed areas. There is virtually no possibility of Indians acquiring European homes, and, conversely, there is little incentive for Europeans to buy the many homes which will become available in areas formerly Indian, since Europeans still have room for expansion within the predominantly European areas.[3]

The evacuation of Indians, therefore, becomes essentially a problem of rehousing, and of the re-establishment of community facilities. In 1943 the housing needs of the Indian population for the next ten years were estimated as 17,600 houses. The position was certainly not less acute when the City Council framed its Group Areas proposals, and the problem will now be accentuated by the needs of Indians

[1] At the hearings of the Group Areas Board, one of the witnesses for the City Council estimated Indian displacement as 54,000; the estimate of the Natal Indian Congress was 57,639 within the city, and an additional 7,106 outside the city (Memorandum presented to Conference on Group Areas Act, previously cited, p. 20).

[2] The South African Institute of Race Relations, in a memorandum to the Group Areas Board, dated 29th September 1952, estimated that there would be a redistribution from Indians to Europeans of property to a value of over £8,500,000. Our own estimate, for the Technical Sub-Committee's original proposals, was £6,000,000 (p. 192).

[3] Indian homes in predominantly European areas would certainly be in demand. It is difficult to assess the probable effects of the Group Areas proposals on the property market. The values of properties in Indian areas are already inflated. Property values in European areas are almost certain to fall, though there may be some gains in racially mixed areas and marginal areas, which are converted to European occupation.

displaced from their homes. The same situation arises with
regard to Indian schools. Most of these schools have been
built on the basis that the Indians purchase the land and
contribute half the cost of building, and even then, between
11,000 and 12,000 Indian children could not be admitted
to Natal schools in 1956, while over 10,000 Indian children
attend 'platoon' (or afternoon) schools. On a provincial
authority, which does not as yet meet the needs of Indian
education, there falls the obligation to replace, in Durban
alone, twenty-two schools, serving about one-quarter of the
school-going population of Durban.[1] And we have still not
taken account of Temples, Mosques, and community halls,
nor of shops and factories, which will presumably also be
affected by the reservation of Indian residential areas for
other groups. It is clear that the sensitivity of the City
Council to the different pressures from organized European
groups has thrown to the Europeans areas they do not want
and will not use, and imposed obligations they cannot
seriously hope to discharge.

In the case of the Coloureds, the City Council eliminated
the Sub-Committee's original suggestion for a Coloured zone
north of the Umgeni River, and decided to retain the existing
Coloured Housing Scheme at Sparks Road, west of the
Central Ridge. The scheme comprised at that time only
about eighty-four houses, but the City Council proposed
that the area should be expanded into a Coloured racial zone
by the removal of some 10,500 Indians. Indeed, both the
zones proposed by the City Council for Coloureds (Figure 24)
impose sacrifice on the Indians.

At the hearings of the Group Areas Board, the City
Council's representative argued for the sympathetic treatment of Coloureds: 'we are dealing with a little people and
should not engender in them a feeling that they are being

[1] On the basis of the 1955 enrolment. The only careful study of the effects
of the Group Areas proposals on Indian education in Durban was carried out
by Dr S. Cooppan, and the figures quoted are from his paper on 'The Implications of the Group Areas Act for Indian Education', previously cited.

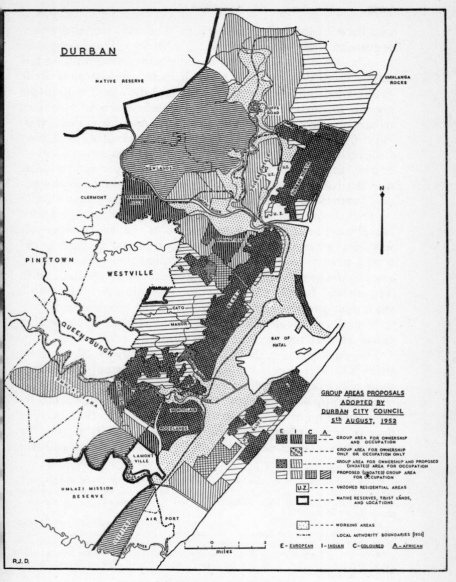

FIGURE 24: ALL RACES

sacrificed to the two major groups'.[1] Demographically the argument was correct, but not politically. The Coloureds have a small municipal vote and, more important, some advocates within the City Council itself. This fact, as well as the small numbers of Coloureds and the absence of antagonism towards them, accounts for their more considerate treatment, at the expense of Indians. And even then, the City Council's plan calls for the displacement of 6,700 Coloureds (40·63 per cent of the 1951 population).

The 'little peoples' of Durban, politically, are the Indians and Africans. The Indians also organized protest meetings, and expressed extreme indignation at the 'uprooting' of settled communities. They appealed for sympathetic recognition of human attachments to homes, places of worship, graveyards, and they discussed the launching of a new passive resistance movement, modelled on the resistance to the so-called 'Ghetto' Act of 1946—the Asiatic Land Tenure and Indian Representation Act. It was all in vain, since their protests and appeals lacked the eloquence of the vote and conflicted with European interests. The main sacrifices were imposed on the Indians.

The Africans, for their part, were relatively silent, but there is little reason to suppose that protest would have been more effective, and their zones fall, as in the Sub-Committee's original proposals, substantially outside the city boundaries (compare Figure 24, p. 201, with Figure 21, p. 189). Over 80,000 Africans may be displaced under the City Council's plan,[2] and it seems probable that Government policy will be

[1] The *Natal Daily News*, 10th August 1953.

[2] The memorandum of the South African Institute of Race Relations, previously cited, shows African displacement as 82,500: the memorandum submitted by the Natal Indian Congress to the Group Areas Conference gives an estimate of 81,886.

The Chesterville location for Africans on the western boundaries of Cato Manor was proposed for European occupation. It was not shown as such on the City Council's map (and is therefore left blank in Figure 24) since the powers of the Group Areas Act do not extend to Urban Native Locations referred to in Section 2 of the Natives (Urban Areas) Consolidation Act, No. 25, of 1945.

directed towards the entire removal of the African population from the city into the peripheral zones.

The present (1956) housing needs of the African population are estimated by the City Council at 16,000 houses for families and 24,000 beds for single persons. If allowance is made for natural increase and increase by migration, then clearly the dimensions of the housing problem will far exceed the resources of the City Council. And we have not taken account of the needs which would arise as the African population develops a more balanced age and sex structure. In all probability the City Council will be obliged to limit its obligations, providing partly houses of modest standard, and partly only building sites and a minimum of municipal services; much of the burden of home-building is likely to fall on the people themselves. Even with assistance from the City Council in the way of building materials and loans, many of the homes are likely to be shack dwellings. Portion of the northern African zone, falling outside the city boundary and far removed from the main industrial centre, is now being developed, and 2,000 Indians are threatened with removal. The plans follow the pattern of neighbourhood planning in England, two of the ten 'neighbourhood units', however, being for single men housed in cottage hostels.

Against this background the carefully devised criteria and procedures of the Technical Sub-Committee appear to be of minor relevance. In its memorandum to the Group Areas Board, the City Council comments on the considerations which governed its zoning proposals, *inter alia*, 'the prime desirability of avoiding population movements as far as possible', and then adds: 'it is inevitable that these various considerations should sometimes conflict with one another, and in such cases, it is a matter of nice judgment which is to prevail.'[1]

There may be some substance to the allegation made by Non-Europeans that this 'nice judgment' was always

[1] Explanatory Memorandum on Group Areas Proposals adopted by Durban City Council, 5th August 1952, p. 19.

exercised for the benefit of Europeans. It is unnecessary, however, to analyse under what circumstances the City Council varied the application of its planning criteria, since we can explain adequately almost all the City Council's proposals for Europeans without reference to any of its planning criteria. The proposals quite simply and directly secure the preservation of European settlements and the extension of European holdings of desirable land at the expense of Non-Europeans. We are not suggesting that the criteria had *no* relevance at all. Nor are we suggesting that the City Council wrote around to European groups, asking what parts of Durban they would like, and then framed a plan to satisfy all their desires. But the effect was much the same, given the non-representative character of the City Council. At local Government level, the Group Areas Act set in motion an inevitable political process, which lavishly tailored racial zones to the needs and desires of organized European groups.

At national level, the Government has not yet proclaimed Group Areas for Durban. Most of the recommendations of the Government-appointed Group Areas Board are, however, already known, and these involve a substantial acceptance of the City Council's proposals. Initially the Planning and Reference Committee, also Government-appointed, expressed reservations about some aspects of the City Council's plan. During the course of the hearings, however, most of these difficulties were resolved, the Committee and the City Council arriving at substantial agreement on the City Council's plan. The Committee, for example, abandoned its objection to the creation of a European pocket on the southern section of the ridge (Woodlands and Montclair), subject to the City Council's agreement that the boundary of the southern Indian zone should be extended to the Umhlatuzana River.[1] Ecologically

---

[1] This would involve the addition to the Indian zone of the area immediately west of Woodlands and Montclair (Figure 23, p. 197).

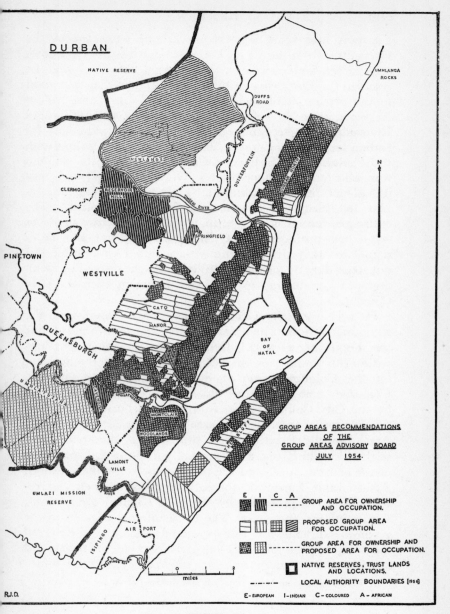

DURBAN

NATIVE RESERVE

UMHLANGA
ROCKS

DUFFS
ROAD

NEWLANDS

DUIKERFONTEIN

CLERMONT

RESERVOIR
HILLS

UMGENI RIVER

SPRINGFIELD

PINETOWN

WESTVILLE

CATO

MANOR

QUEENSBURGH

BAY
OF
NATAL

UMHLATUZANA

MONTCLAIR

THE BLUFF

WOODLANDS

GROUP AREAS RECOMMENDATIONS
OF THE
GROUP AREAS ADVISORY BOARD
JULY 1954.

LAMONT
VILLE

UMLAZI MISSION
RESERVE

AIR PORT

ISIPINGO

ISIPINGO RIVER

0   1   2
miles

E   I   C   A

GROUP AREA FOR OWNERSHIP
AND OCCUPATION.

PROPOSED GROUP AREA
FOR OCCUPATION.

GROUP AREA FOR OWNERSHIP AND
PROPOSED AREA FOR OCCUPATION.

NATIVE RESERVES, TRUST LANDS
AND LOCATIONS.

LOCAL AUTHORITY BOUNDARIES [1956]

E - EUROPEAN   I - INDIAN   C - COLOURED   A - AFRICAN

R.J.D.

FIGURE 25

the most interesting concession was one extracted by the Committee from the City Council, that Riverside (in tract 5 on the sea-front north of the Umgeni River) should be reserved for Europeans. Only a few years earlier, pursuant to the provisions of the Asiatic Land Tenure and Indian Representation Act of 1946, the claims of the Indians in Riverside were recognized, the area being indicated for Indian settlement. Yet now, as a result of its discussions with the Planning and Reference Committee, the City Council was able to announce to the Group Areas Board that it had accepted the Committee's proposal for the reservation to Europeans of this old Indian settlement. The entire residential coastal strip north of the Umgeni River was thus proposed as a European reservation. It is significant that the Government-appointed Committee did not consider it necessary to consult the Non-European organizations in any way on its agreement with the City Council.

In July 1954 the Group Areas Board announced the recommendations it had made to the Minister of the Interior (see Figure 25, p. 205).[1] Decision on the African locations within the boundaries was deferred, as was also the decision on the Coloured zone at Sparks Road. The southern Coloured zone was, however, recommended as proposed by the City Council, apart from a small portion adjoining the European area. In the case of the Indians the Group Areas Board deferred decision in respect of the areas north of the Umgeni River, a substantial portion of the zone west of the central ridge, and the corridor between the southern African and European zones, and recommended the remaining areas proposed by the City Council for Indians, with some modifications. The main interest attaches to the recommendations for Europeans. Decision was deferred only in respect of land on the extreme northern and south-western boundaries. For the rest, apart from minor

---

[1] Recommended areas are hatched, and deferred areas are left blank.

adjustments, the Group Areas Board accepted all the City Council's proposals for European Group Areas.

In broad outline, then, the Board has followed the City Council's plan. It seems doubtful whether its recommendations were materially influenced by the public hearings, the invitations to interested parties to submit plans, the examination and cross-examination of witnesses, and the whole paraphernalia of quasi-judicial process. The decisions of the Board could have been reached, substantially if not in full detail, by discussion between its representatives and the City Council.

The main burden of sacrifice is imposed on the Indians, though it is possible that the Board may still mitigate this consequence by its treatment of the deferred areas, or of the established Indian communities in the working zones, more particularly in the Old Borough. But, whatever the final recommendations, the Board has already accepted the principle of reserving the residential core of Durban for Europeans.

The recommendations carry forward the distinction between the Old Borough and the Added Areas in a new form. Originally, Non-Europeans had settled predominantly in the undeveloped areas outside the city boundaries, though retaining substantial settlements within the Old Borough. The peripheral areas were later incorporated into the Added Areas of the city. Now the same process is deliberately planned. The Group Areas proposals involve the incorporation of additional undeveloped land, and a large proportion of the Non-European population will be redistributed into these new Added Areas, leaving developed land within the present boundaries of the city for European expansion. The main difference is that, in the past, Non-Europeans settled voluntarily in the peripheral areas, whereas, under the provisions of the Group Areas Act as applied to Durban, they will be under compulsion to move into even more peripheral settlements beyond the city boundaries.

The effect of the Group Areas plans is therefore to eliminate Non-European competition for the land of

Durban. This is the inevitable consequence of the wide powers conferred by the Group Areas Act within a political structure which vests the effective monopoly of power in the European group. The broad agreement between the proposals of the City Council and the recommendations of the Group Areas Board is an index of the extent to which the same political pressures operate at local and national levels.

In May 1957 the Group Areas Board again met in Durban to hear evidence in regard to the deferred areas. The City Council's proposals involved some changes from its original plans, namely:—

an allocation of land to Indians and Coloureds in the southern coastal area of the Bluff; a consolidation of the European area in the Umhlatuzana-Umbilo inter-fluve with the areas north and south; a straightening of the boundaries, and the creation of a buffer zone, between the Indian, Coloured and European areas, west of the Central Berea Ridge; an allocation of undeveloped land to Indians and Coloureds towards the western boundary in the Umgeni valley area; the expansion, to the North Coast railway line, of the European area north of the Umgeni River; and the reservation for Coloureds of portion of the Duikerfontein area, north of the Umgeni River, coupled with the suggestion that the remainder of the area should be left unzoned. Duikerfontein, apart from two strips along the main road, had originally been proposed for Indians, and includes one of the best Indian suburbs.

The effect, on balance, was a further proposed encroachment on Indian holdings for the benefit of other groups, the extension of European holdings by the addition of previously unzoned land, and a more generous provision for Coloureds.

Plans have not yet been published for the racial zoning of the working areas, of the industrial and commercial centres, but Indians fear that their interests will inevitably be sacrificed in areas of high property values. Throughout the course of Group Areas development in Durban, the general pattern of the Council's policy has been the progressive redistribution of Indian property interests. It is expressed in the plans submitted by the Council at the two hearings of the Group Areas Board, in its policies with regard to the issue of permits, and in its attempts to secure the conversion to industrial, or 'White', use, of the closely settled Indian suburb of Clairwood. And it reflects directly and simply the political realities of the situation.

There may, however, be some revision of plans by the Durban City Council. Towards the end of 1957 the Government announced proposals for the amendment of the Group Areas Development Act, which the Durban City Council opposed, as interfering with the autonomy of local authorities and imposing on them the financial burden of carrying out the Government's own 'apartheid' plans. This rift in the close harmony about Group Areas may allow new insights into the nature of the policy, not only of the Government, but also of the Durban City Council. At the same time there has been some concern about the moral implications of the Group Areas proposals, the effect on rates of the high cost of population displacement, and the possibility of carrying out the plans at all unless more adequate provision is made for Indian needs. The proposals may be revised to the extent of allowing Indians to remain, and perhaps expand, in some of their peripheral areas, proposed for Europeans, but not wanted by them. Any more fundamental revision would run counter to the firmly established policy of Europeans in Durban towards Indians, entrenched as this policy is by the whole structure of South African society.

o

CHAPTER VIII

PROSPECT

We have not dealt with Group Areas proposals throughout the country, nor with the general legislative context of the Group Areas Act. A factual account of the different plans is given in Muriel Horrell, *The Group Areas Act—Its Effect on Human Beings* (South African Institute of Race Relations, 1956), and an interpretation of the legislative framework in Leo Kuper, *Passive Resistance in South Africa* (Jonathan Cape, 1956, chapter II).

The latter study interprets the Group Areas Act as part of a co-ordinated plan for white domination, by the avoidance of race contact on a basis of equality, and by the breakdown of the numerically predominant Non-Europeans into separate and mutually exclusive communities. For the purposes of this analysis, we have taken the objective of the Group Areas Act as announced, namely the promotion of racial harmony by the avoidance of contact. Whatever the motives of the Government, the races are to be separated into Group Areas, and our present concern is with the research problems arising from racial separation.

MASTER plans for racial segregation are in preparation throughout the country, and they are to be carried out, as proclamations are made in the different areas. The plans constitute a vast series of experiments of a most unusual type in urban ecology and race relations, and under conditions which vary in different areas. As such, they provide a field of research which may contribute generally to sociological theory, and specifically to the evaluation of public policy in South Africa. For the study of these experiments, we need a picture of the situation prior to the proclamation of Group Areas. Our own inquiry was designed with this end in view, to give the ecological and demographic information which would serve as a basis for the analysis of the processes and results of urban change initiated by racial zoning in Durban.

The proposals of the Durban City Council, as we have seen, call for the incorporation within the city of undeveloped land, and the settlement on it of Indians and Africans. The same pattern has evolved also in other towns. It provides an easy solution for the allocation of living room to Non-Europeans, without sacrifice by Europeans. Indeed, as we have seen, it enables Europeans to extend their holdings of land and to spread more widely over the existing areas of the city.

Taking South Africa as a whole—rural and urban areas—the effects of this policy are to stimulate a drive for territorial expansion, not so much for the sake of markets in the Imperialist tradition, as for land for Non-European settlement. In the same way that the incorporation of undeveloped land provides an ideal solution for some European Town Councils, so, too, the incorporation of undeveloped territories beyond the borders of South Africa would provide an ideal solution for the Government. The incorporation of the British Protectorates, for example, would assist the Government to find additional living space for Non-Europeans, without sacrifice by Europeans.

In the urban areas the effects of the Group Areas Act will thus be to stimulate a process of dispersion. This is already a marked characteristic of South African Town Planning, but it will be accentuated by systematic racial zoning. Europeans will be more sparsely settled within the existing towns, while Non-European settlements will be sited increasingly on undeveloped land, peripheral to the town and remote from the main centre.

The study of these Non-European dormitory or satellite townships is a matter of great urgency in terms of public policy. Costs of development will certainly be high, on account of distance from the main service centres. The same political process which ensures the reservation of the more desirable land for Europeans may be expected also to limit expenditure on Non-European areas, particularly since the concept of separate development implies, to some extent, that Non-Europeans should carry the financial responsibility for the development of their own areas. Displacement under the Group Areas Act will magnify the present acute housing shortage, while the increased difficulties of the journey to work will severely limit the energy and resources of the Non-Europeans for development work. These factors, coupled with the poverty of the Non-Europeans and their consequent inability to make an effective financial contribution, must inevitably bring about a situation in which the great majority of the Non-European settlements will have a low standard, not only of urban amenities, but of the basic necessities.

Many of the Non-European urban settlements are, at present, of this type, peripheral and indeed little more than shanty townships, though there are also well-planned locations and housing projects. Comparison between these different types of settlement (as, for example, in Durban, the locations of Lamontville and Chesterville on the one hand, and the shack habitations of Cato Manor on the other) will assist in the analysis of the effects of the general environment of a township area on the mode of life of its people. At the same time we need studies of newly established racial zones (such as the Duffs Road Township for Africans) from the first stages of planning. How crucial are the township environmental factors as compared with the political and economic relations between white and non-white? Are we, in fact, creating separate residential areas in which Non-European groups 'will be able to give expression to their full cultural and soul life'?[1] Or are we building 'pariah'

---

[1] One of the positive benefits claimed for racial zoning is that it insulates the non-Whites against the humiliations and inequalities inevitable in situations of contact, by providing the opportunity for each group to develop its special potentialities in its own separate racial area. 'Hon. members will realize what it must mean to those groups, always to have to adopt an inferior attitude, an attitude of inferiority towards the Europeans, to stand back for the Europeans,

settlements, characterized by high crime rates and other indices of social disorganization? And, if so, then to what extent are these internal conflicts an expression of suppressed hostility towards Europeans, and under what conditions may they be resolved by overt aggression against this white out-group?

Within the present boundaries of the towns, the conversion of Non-European areas to European presents many problems of sociological interest. Group Areas proposals, as in Durban, involve a planned invasion by a dominant group of suburbs inhabited by subordinate groups. Some of these suburbs have sufficient advantages to outweigh the stigma which Europeans attach to areas occupied by Non-Europeans. In other suburbs blight will inevitably descend, unless steps are taken to improve the amenities and residential status of the areas, so as to attract Europeans. How will these processes of planned conversion compare with the processes in the unplanned invasions and successions reported in many American studies?

To a large extent the present ecological distribution of the races is a distribution of income groups. Race differences and economic differences tend to coincide, with the poorer Non-European groups living in the Alluvial Flats and the Inland Hilly Region, and the wealthier European groups on the seaward-facing slopes, though there are some marked exceptions, as, for example, in the concentration of wealthier Indians on the lower slopes of the Central Berea Ridge. Presumably the conversion of Non-European areas will result in the substitution of an ecological distribution based clearly on class differences within the European community. In place of an 'encirclement' of Europeans

where they live alongside the Europeans, but if we place them in separate residential areas, they will be able to give expression to their full cultural and soul life, and that is why we say that separate residential areas must be established.' (The Minister of the Interior at the conclusion of the second hearing of the Group Areas Bill, Hansard, *House of Assembly Debates*, vols. 70–3, 31st May 1950, p. 7825).

by Non-Europeans, there may now be an 'encirclement' of upper class by lower class. What would be the effect on ecological patterns of social disorganization? Does the presence of middle-class Indian families in the transitional zone of the Old Borough help to stabilize the area? And, when they leave, will new ecological patterns of delinquency, crime, and divorce emerge? What is the relationship between racial mixture in residential areas, and the incidence of social disorganization among the different racial groups living there?

Up to the present we have been assuming that Group Areas proposals will be carried out as planned. This may be so in many towns: it seems highly improbable in a city such as Durban. The First 'Penetration' Commission emphasized the attachment of Indians to their land—'it is the outward visible sign of the inward spiritual grace of wealth'—and expressed the opinion that Indian opposition to compulsory segregation would never be overcome.[1] The Asiatic Land Tenure and Indian Representation Act of 1946 (the 'Ghetto' Act) was followed by a Passive Resistance movement in Durban—the first since Mahatma Gandhi left South Africa—and over 2,000 Indians were sentenced to terms of imprisonment. In 1952 the South African Indian Congress joined the African National Congress in a Civil Disobedience Campaign, directed primarily, so far as the Indians were concerned, against the Group Areas Act.

In the case of the Africans, they have been drawn to the city as a result of industrial development and rural impoverishment. It is probable that they will continue to enter the city, whatever regulations are passed to control their influx, and they will find accommodation where they can, whatever the patterns of racial zoning. From both these groups, then, Indians and Africans, but particularly Indians, there will be resistance to a neat ordering into peripheral racial zones, and the strength and security of this inevitable resistance lie in the large numbers involved. Every section of the Indian

---

[1] *Report of the First Indian 'Penetration' Commission*, p. 74.

population, from the wealthiest of merchants to the poorest of labourers, is affected by Group Areas plans. Moreover, if the racial zoning interferes with the availability and efficiency of the labour supply, then the industrialists themselves will exert pressure for the relaxation of controls and the modification of plans.

If we are correct in stating that the cost of developing the racial zones so as to attract displaced Non-Europeans will exceed the resources of the City Council and seem too high a charge for the benefits of total segregation; and if the accession of new land to Europeans in Durban far exceeds their requirements and may affect the property market adversely; then it seems likely that the Europeans will ask for a revision of the plans. They will either withdraw the proposals for conversion of some of the Indian areas, or refrain from implementing racial conversion in these areas, and content themselves with the removal of Indians from the more coveted suburbs. The redistribution of population will certainly be less radical than the City Council's proposals. The research problem, however, is not the specific detail of the modification of the City Council's plans, but the limitations on the planner's total blue-prints for living— limitations which arise from the fact that there is a 'human element' involved, that human beings are not merely counters on a checkers board.

Research into the race-relations aspects of Group Areas is even more urgent. The basic problem is the effect of contact on race relations, and the American studies of inter-racial housing projects might well serve as a model. In particular, the conclusion that proximity promotes contact and more favourable beliefs and attitudes[1] should be

[1] Wilner, Walkley and Cook, *Human Relations in Inter-racial Housing* (University of Minnesota Press, 1955). The effect of proximity on attitudes was studied incidentally in a survey of an old African location in Durban: the results were inconclusive (*The Baumannville Community*, Institute for Social Research, University of Natal, 1955, pp. 183–6). Miss Margo Phillips, also of the University of Natal, is at present investigating the same problem in a racially mixed area on the lower slopes of the Central Berea Ridge.

tested in the very different environment of South African
life. This would give some insight into the significance of
the conditions which govern the contact—the significance,
for example, of the attitudes towards inter-racial contact,
approving as in some of the American housing projects, or
disapproving as in South Africa. In addition, such a study
would provide data for the critical analysis of the basic
assumption of the Group Areas Act, that contact gives rise
to conflict.[1]

Parallel studies of changes in attitude would be of great
value. Instead of comparing the attitudes of different
residents—those in contact and those not in contact with
members of another race—we would study changes in
attitude of the same resident over a period of time. What is
the effect on the racial attitudes of residents when they are
moved from areas of mixed racial living into a racial zone?
Does isolation from contact stimulate suspicion and hostility,
as many sociologists would expect, or does it, under the

[1] There is an ambivalence in the attitude to the consequences of contact,
as shown in the question posed by the Prime Minister during the Parliamentary
debate on Group Areas. 'What is the use of having a law to deal with mixed
marriages if we have conditions . . . where Europeans and Non-Europeans
live alongside each other, and associate with each other, where the children
play together in the streets and where the colour feelings of the Europeans are
becoming dulled, and where the colour sense, which is the white man's protection, disappears completely. What is the use in such circumstances to try
to prevent mixed marriages?' (Hansard, *House of Assembly Debates*, p. 7724.)
This statement places marriage, neighbour relations and children's play
groups in the same class of social phenomena—they are all contacts on the
basis of equality—and the Prime Minister envisaged, as a result of this type of
contact, the loss of a sense of colour or racial identity by the white group.
He was, in fact, asserting that the perception of racial difference would weaken
with intimate contact, and that in this way the white group would lose its
identity by a process of fusion. Far from creating racial conflict, inter-racial
contact on a basis of equality may dull the sense of colour, and hence the
relevance of racial identity for social relationships. There are thus two routes
to ultimate racial harmony—by integration, through multiplying points of
intimate equal contact, and by separation, through segregation and the reduction of points of contact. Both contact and the avoidance of contact, promote
harmony, but in different ways, and the harmony of contact, through equality
and fusion, is the most powerful argument for avoiding contact. The Group
Areas Act, and separation generally, are seen as a means for protecting the
white man from absorption into, or subordination by, the Non-European
majority.

conditions of South African society, promote more tolerant attitudes?

There are at present, and there will be for years to come, and no doubt permanently, many mixed racial areas in South Africa, where these problems of contact can be analysed. Our study throws no light on them, but it does suggest some possible consequences for race relations of proposals to avoid contact by the machinery of Group Areas.

Attitudes which are rewarding tend to be reinforced. The Group Areas Act is rewarding to Europeans and, in operating the Act, they tend to make use of its basic assumptions. The effect is, therefore, to implant or strengthen the belief, in the minds of Europeans, that race contact is undesirable. Thus, the representative of the Durban North Ratepayers' Association based his case for the removal of Indians from Riverside and Prospect Hall on the ground, *inter alia*, that European and Indian children played together in the street. This, he declared, hardly made for racial harmony. Yet he was not able to cite a single instance of conflict resulting from these contacts, though he commented that there was some resentment.

In suggesting that motives of personal gain predispose Europeans to accept the theory that inter-racial contact is a source of conflict, we do not wish to imply that other motives, and indeed considerations of equity, have no force. This study, however, demonstrates, in the case of Durban, that the system of 'partial democracy' (for want of a better term) gives maximum play to the pursuit of material gain, precisely *because* the system operates by democratic procedures for the minority who enjoy the vote.

Ratepayers' Associations are organized to promote their property interests by mass meetings and other agitation, and by pressure on their Council representatives. Since other Ratepayers' Associations proceed in the same way, there results an accommodation of competing interests. This is a democratic way of arriving at a rough approximation to justice. It can only work, however, when each of the organized groups has an equal opportunity to promote its interests. Where, as in most South African towns, only the European residents have an effective voice in the affairs of the Council, the probable result is not an accommodation of competing interests but satisfaction of European demands at the expense of Non-Europeans. This is, in fact, what happened in Durban. Under the City Council's proposals, European settlements will be preserved and extended, while Non-European settlements will be removed. Europeans have security, Non-Europeans live in insecurity. And feelings of security and insecurity are generally assumed to affect race prejudice.

Many observers comment that the attitudes of the Europeans in Durban to Indians are more favourable as a result of the Group Areas Act. One of the leaders of the Natal Indian Organization agreed with this assessment, explaining it as a natural consequence of the fact that the Group Areas Act gives Europeans all that they want.[1] This may be too easy an explanation. Agitation against the Indians in Durban has always been cyclical; it was never maintained for any length of time at fever heat. Moreover, feelings of security or insecurity are not necessarily related to the facts: a ruling group may feel secure on the verge of revolution, or insecure when there is little threat to its privileged position, as was the case in the agitation against Indians which preceded the First 'Penetration' Commission. And the existence of wide and unused powers under the Group Areas Act may make Europeans increasingly sensitive to hypothetical threats against their security.

In the case of the Non-Europeans, their leaders are certainly keenly conscious of insecurity. The phrase 'Forever Hamba' ('Forever Go'), used in the African

---

[1] A leading City Councillor also emphasized security to Europeans when he appealed to them to try and change their attitudes towards the Non-Europeans, 'now that we have complete protection' (*Natal Mercury*, 31st August 1951).

newspaper *Ilanga Lase*, Natal, and applied by one of the leaders of the African National Congress to Government policy with reference to his people, graphically describes this insecurity. The Indians have greater reason to feel insecure in Durban, since areas which were indicated for Indian settlement under the provisions of the Asiatic Land Tenure and Indian Representation Act of 1946, and some of the areas which were predominantly Indian many years before the First 'Penetration' Commission, are now proposed for European occupation.

The City Council of Durban is well aware of the insecurity which its Group Areas proposals have caused the Non-European population, and it has urged on the Government the need for an early proclamation of Group Areas as a means of alleviating this insecurity. The proclamations will, however, mean the progressive dissolution of settled communities, while at present there is some hope of a Government reprieve. Moreover, there is no possibility of security in Group Areas; the Group Areas Act and the Group Areas Development Act are the very instruments, and the continuing instruments, for insecurity, since they set aside common-law rights and provide the means for the removal of whole communities. There can be no guarantee that the Non-Europeans will be secure in their Group Areas.

The effects of insecurity, arising from the Group Areas Act, have not been studied. Non-Europeans are largely dependent on Europeans for employment, education, housing and municipal amenities. This dependence, combined with insecurity, appears to make for docility among many Non-Europeans. Some, however, increasingly reject the white man and his rule, and think in terms of revolutionary change.

There are two circumstances in the mechanism of Group Areas which contribute to the radical rejection of the white man. First, racial zoning affects fundamental human values, the attachment of men to their homes and communities, and these values are apparently disregarded in a light-hearted manner. Second, the link between the fate of Non-Europeans and the dispensations of Europeans is made manifest. Prior to the Group Areas Act, the racial ecology of a city might have been regarded, in some small measure, as an expression of natural causes, an act of God. Now, however, the public hearings of the Group Areas Board are an almost theatrical demonstration of European responsibility. Patently, any injustice in the distribution of land is the deliberate act of Europeans.

The sacrifices demanded of the different racial groups in Durban correspond to the racial hierarchy, as between Europeans, Coloureds and Indians. The Europeans are protected, indeed rewarded; the major sacrifice is demanded of Indians; while the Coloureds occupy an intermediate position. This inequality may introduce an ambiguity in the relations of Coloureds and Indians. Indians are aware that the Coloureds are not the agents of their displacement, but may feel resentment against them as the instruments by which settled communities are disrupted. And the Coloureds' own reaction to their role as the passive means of Indian discomfiture cannot fail to affect the relations of the two groups. In the perception of the European role, however, there can be no ambiguity at all. The Europeans take the stage as the arbiters of Non-European destiny.

Racial zoning, if it is to be just, demands sacrifices from Europeans. This study of Group Areas in Durban is a case study of the possibility of sacrifice where the opportunity for material gain is linked with the monopoly of power. It demonstrates, in a particular instance, that the political process was such that, far from requiring sacrifice by the Europeans, the Group Areas Act converted political power to material gain. The present inequality in the distribution of resources is accentuated by inequality in sacrifice. Indians, in particular, feel that the racial zoning in Durban is gravely unjust, and a sense of injustice is certainly a major

threat to harmonious race relations. This the Minister of
the Interior clearly perceived, when he declared, at the conclusion of the Parliamentary debate on the second reading
of the Group Areas Bill:

> '*I also want to say this, that no policy which is not based
> on justice has any prospect of success.*'

APPENDIX A

Distribution of Incomes of Europeans, Coloureds and Indians, and Calculation of Mean and *Per Capita* Incomes of African Population

TABLE IX

ANNUAL INCOMES OF THE EUROPEAN, COLOURED AND INDIAN POPULATIONS IN DURBAN: 1951 CENSUS

Income in £ per annum	Europeans			Coloureds			Indians		
	Males	Females	Total	Males	Females	Total	Males	Females	Total
No Income	19,580	44,208	63,788	4,549	6,555	11,104	44,890	68,739	113,629
Under £50	374	1,129	1,503	175	391	566	2,118	1,223	3,341
50– 99	1,101	2,735	3,836	319	598	917	5,881	812	6,693
100– 149	1,878	2,165	4,043	523	562	1,085	7,723	408	8,131
150– 199	1,677	2,503	4,180	345	385	730	4,709	208	4,917
200– 249	2,113	3,387	5,500	443	149	592	3,175	85	3,260
250– 299	1,821	2,649	4,470	248	33	281	1,488	28	1,516
300– 349	2,201	2,689	4,890	217	13	230	1,091	27	1,118
350– 399	2,488	1,941	4,429	138	9	147	914	12	926
400– 499	5,643	1,765	7,408	327	2	329	776	16	792
500– 599	6,799	827	7,626	206	2	208	382	10	392
600– 799	9,256	553	9,809	116	2	118	309	16	325
800– 999	3,532	240	3,772	12	—	12	114	3	117
1,000–1,499	2,707	234	2,941	3	—	3	153	7	160
1,500–1,999	850	107	957	1	—	1	77	4	81
2,000–2,499	480	52	532	1	—	1	33	—	33
2,500–2,999	278	34	312	—	—	—	14	—	14
3,000–3,999	277	39	316	—	—	—	12	—	12
4,000–4,999	110	14	124	—	—	—	6	—	6
5,000 and over	300	20	320	—	—	—	8	—	8
Unspecified	394	143	537	98	67	165	630	82	712
TOTAL .	63,859	67,434	131,293	7,721	8,768	16,489	74,503	71,680	146,183

P

TABLE X

PERCENTAGE DISTRIBUTION OF THE ANNUAL INCOMES OF THE EUROPEAN, COLOURED AND INDIAN POPULATIONS IN DURBAN: 1951 CENSUS

Income in £ per annum	Europeans			Coloureds			Indians		
	Males	Females	Total	Males	Females	Total	Males	Females	Total
No Income	14·91	33·67	48·58	27·59	39·75	67·34	30·71	47·02	77·73
Under £50	0·28	0·86	1·14	1·06	2·37	3·43	1·45	0·84	2·29
50– 99	0·84	2·08	2·92	1·93	3·63	5·56	4·02	0·56	4·58
100– 149	1·43	1·65	3·08	3·17	3·41	6·58	5·28	0·28	5·56
150– 199	1·27	1·91	3·18	2·09	2·34	4·43	3·22	0·14	3·36
200– 249	1·61	2·58	4·19	2·69	0·90	3·59	2·17	0·06	2·23
250– 299	1·38	2·02	3·40	1·50	0·20	1·70	1·02	0·02	1·04
300– 349	1·67	2·05	3·72	1·31	0·08	1·39	0·74	0·02	0·76
350– 399	1·89	1·48	3·37	0·84	0·05	0·89	0·62	0·01	0·63
400– 499	4·31	1·34	5·65	1·99	0·01	2·00	0·53	0·01	0·54
500– 599	5·19	0·63	5·82	1·25	0·01	1·26	0·26	0·01	0·27
600– 799	7·06	0·42	7·48	0·71	0·01	0·72	0·21	0·01	0·22
800– 999	2·69	0·18	2·87	0·07	—	0·07	0·08	0·00	0·08
1,000–1,499	2·06	0·18	2·24	0·02	0·02	—	0·10	0·01	0·11
1,500–1,999	0·65	0·08	0·73	0·01	0·01	—	0·05	0·01	0·06
2,000–2,499	0·37	0·04	0·41	0·01	0·01	—	0·02	—	0·02
2,500–2,999	0·21	0·03	0·24	—	—	—	0·01	—	0·01
3,000–3,999	0·21	0·03	0·24	—	—	—	0·01	—	0·01
4,000–4,999	0·08	0·01	0·09	—	—	—	0·00	—	0·00
5,000 and over	0·22	0·02	0·24	—	—	—	0·01	—	0·01
Unspecified	0·30	0·11	0·41	0·59	0·41	1·00	0·43	0·06	0·49
TOTAL	48·63	51·37	100·00	46·83	53·17	100·00	50·94	49·06	100·00

ESTIMATE OF THE MEAN AND *PER CAPITA* INCOMES OF THE AFRICAN POPULATION OF DURBAN, 1951

Our estimate of the total income of African workers is arrived at as follows:

(1) *Male Workers in Industry, Commerce, Government and Municipal Service*

In July 1950 the National Development Foundation (Durban Centre) collected data in regard to the earnings of African males employed in Durban, in commerce, industry, government and municipal service.[1] The survey covered about 58 per cent of African male workers in commerce and industry, and 97 per cent in government and municipal service. Their mean income (excluding overtime payment and the cash value of rations) was £121·57 per annum.[2] On the assumptions that:

(a) the survey categories correspond to the Census categories of manufacturing, construction, electricity, gas, water and sanitary service, commerce, transport, storage and communication, and services excluding domestic service [3] (see Table I);

(b) the income of the workers was roughly the same at the time of the 1951 Census as in July 1950; and

[1] H. R. Burrows, 'Native Incomes, Housing and the Cost of Living', *S.A. Journal of Economics*, vol. 19, no. 4 (December 1951), pp. 349 et seq.

[2] Our own calculation, based on the distribution of income given in the Foundation's survey. We have assumed that the mid-point of the monthly income class of £15 and over was £20.

[3] The Census of Industrial Distribution, 1951 Census, gives the total number of African males employed in the services as 28,196, of whom 13,030 were domestic servants.

(*c*) the survey sample was representative;

we estimate the total annual cash income of the 66,231 African male workers[1] in the categories listed in (*a*) above, as about £8,051,808

(2) *Domestic Servants*

Estimates of the mean income of African male domestic servants, given by officials of the Durban Labour Bureau, varied from £5 to £7 or £8 per month. The Institute for Social Research of the University of Natal, in a study of the small Durban location of Baumannville, found the mean income of male domestic servants living away from their employers to be £9·06 per month.[2] Since young boys are widely employed at a salary of between £2 to £3 per month, with food and quarters, an overall average of about £6 10s. od. per month is probably a reasonable estimate. Excluding the value of food and quarters, this would yield to the 13,030 male domestic servants a total annual income of about £84,695

Using, as a basis, the figure of £4·64 per month[3] as the average wage of the 15,178 African women domestic servants in Durban, we calculate their total annual income as about .   .   £70,425

Total Annual Income £8,206,928

(3) The above estimate covers 94,439 persons of the 99,375 African workers gainfully employed in 1951. We have not estimated the earnings of

---

[1] In July 1950 there were about 68,400 African male workers in commerce, industry, government and municipal service, and 37,600 in hotels, domestic service and various other undertakings. The Census figures exclude workers employed in Durban but living outside.

[2] W. C. Hallenbeck (ed.), *The Baumannville Community: A Study of the First African Family Location in Durban* (Institute for Social Research, University of Natal, Durban, 1955).

[3] Ibid., p. 116, Table 39.

the small numbers of workers in mining, quarrying and agriculture, nor of women in industry and commerce, and we could not attempt an estimate in the case of activities not adequately described. Assuming that these workers earn, on an average, roughly the same amount as the main body of workers, we estimate *the total annual income of the employed African population* as about   .   .   .   .   . ~~£8,635,875~~ *10,431,374*

and the Mean Annual Income[1] *as about* .   . ~~£87~~ *105*

The above figures make no allowance for the value of food and quarters, nor for income from a variety of sources used to supplement earnings.

(4) Distributed over the total African population of 136,279 persons in Durban, this income yields *an annual* per capita *income* of about   .   . ~~£63~~ *77*
However, many African workers support dependants outside Durban. Assuming that the average amount remitted to these dependants is £25 per annum per worker,[2] *the annual* per capita *income* would be reduced to about   . ~~£45~~ *58*

[1] The residents of Lamontville and Chesterville locations are among the most highly paid of the African population. Mean annual income—based on a survey carried out in 1956 by Mr E. Mayisela of the Economics Department of the University of Natal—is about £157 for workers living in Lamontville and £132 for workers in Chesterville.

[2] Department of Economics, University of Natal, *The African Factory Worker: A Sample Study of the Life and Labour of the Urban African Worker* (Oxford University Press, 1950), pp. 149–51.

APPENDIX B

CENSUS TRACTS   (i)   Enumerators' Sub-Districts in each Census Tract.

(ii)   Racial Composition of Census Tracts (Absolute Numbers and Percentages, including and excluding Non-European Domestic Servants).

(iii)   Census Tracts in each Sociographic Zone.

SPECIAL TABULATION OF 1951 CENSUS DATA — DURBAN

1951 CENSUS ENUMERATORS' SUB-DISTRICTS IN EACH OF THE 36 CENSUS TRACTS

Census Tract No.	*Census Enumerators' Sub-Districts Nos.*
1	180, 200, 201, 202
2	177, 178, 179, 198, 199
3	168, 170, 166, 167, 169, 171, 172
4	165, 173, 174, 175
5	163, 164
6	176, 197, 203, 204, 205, 226, 225
7	30, 31, 195, 196
8	34, 36, 37, 38, 39, 188, 189, 190, 191, 193, 194
9	83, 84, 88, 85
10	86, 87, 89, 185, 187, 192
11	75, 76, 77, 78, 79, 80, 181, 182, 183, 184
12	69, 70, 71, 72, 73, 74, 81, 82, 90, 91, 92, 93, 94, 95, 96, 97, 98, 99, 219
13	45, 46, 47, 48, 49, 50, 64, 68
14	57, 58, 106, 107, 108, 109, 110, 111, 112, 113, 239
15	59, 60, 61, 62, 63, 65, 100, 101, 102, 103, 104, 105
16	54, 55, 56, 66, 67, 114
17	5, 11, 12, 29, 19, 20, 21, 22, 23, 24, 51, 52, 53
18	40, 41, 44, 25, 26, 27, 28, 32, 33, 35, 42, 43
19	4, 6, 7, 8, 9, 10, 13, 14, 15, 16, 17
20	186, 210, 212, 215, 216, 217, 218, 220, 221, 228, 231, 232, 236, 237, 238
21	227, 229, 230
22	207, 208, 209, 211, 213, 214, 233, 234, 235
23	222, 223, 224, 240, 256, 257, 258, 259, 260, 261, 262, 241, 252, 206

Census Tract No.	*Census Enumerators' Sub-Districts Nos.*
24	242, 243, 244, 245, 246, 247, 248, 249, 250, 251, 253, 254, 255
25	127, 129
26	128, 131, 130, 132, 134, 115, 117, 119, 133, 116, 118, 121
27	120, 122
28	150
29	151, 152, 153, 154, 155, 156, 157, 158, 159, 161
30	160, 141
31	139, 142, 144, 146, 148
32	143, 145, 147, 149
33	136, 138, 140, 137
34	123, 124, 125, 126
35	135
36	18, 162, 1, 2, 3

RACIAL COMPOSITION OF CENSUS TRACTS, DURBAN: 1951 CENSUS

Census Tract No.	Europeans	Coloureds	Indians	Africans	Total
1	778	198	4,905	721	6,602
2	5,061	329	252	1,636	7,278
3	7,357	29	140	3,122	10,648
4	771	302	4,964	2,394	8,431
5	43	132	2,389	141	2,705
6	348	732	11,580	2,315	14,975
7	277	128	7,608	13,598	21,611
8	7,122	685	1,576	2,338	11,721
9	2,190	239	1,019	800	4,248
10	5,231	39	123	1,642	7,035
11	5,973	47	82	2,795	8,897
12	13,874	84	229	4,322	18,509
13	3,959	2,176	5,061	1,483	12,679
14	9,801	127	327	3,165	13,420
15	11,232	166	53	2,877	14,328
16	1,791	693	1,008	11,341	14,833
17	13,880	23	132	3,503	17,538
18	1,367	1,484	13,341	2,903	19,095
19	12,042	120	116	2,662	14,940
20	3,325	1,463	11,127	2,752	18,667
21	318	112	9,224	504	10,158
22	206	2,520	11,198	1,301	15,225
23	1,116	997	18,369	3,987	24,469
24	18	507	988	32,235	33,748
25	2,393	117	266	641	3,417
26	5,053	355	5,713	2,610	13,731
27	891	204	2,088	626	3,809
28	6	—	1,591	1,111	2,708
29	43	1,285	16,266	428	18,022
30	210	407	5,950	2,058	8,625
31	6,273	345	3,292	2,817	12,727
32	2,975	24	178	1,607	4,784
33	577	315	4,686	674	6,252
34	3,335	40	5	1,382	4,762
35	49	6	6	9,827	9,888
36	1,408	59	331	7,961	9,759
Total	131,293	16,489	146,183	136,279	430,244

RACIAL COMPOSITION OF CENSUS TRACTS, (EXCLUDING NON-EUROPEAN DOMESTIC SERVANTS IN PRIVATE HOUSEHOLDS), DURBAN: 1951 CENSUS

Census Tract No.	Europeans	Coloureds	Indians	Africans	Total
1	778	193	4,866	537	6,374
2	5,061	319	239	772	6,391
3	7,357	8	127	463	7,955
4	771	301	4,938	2,149	8,159
5	43	127	2,380	115	2,665
6	348	723	11,556	2,194	14,821
7	277	126	7,600	13,095	21,098
8	7,122	667	1,559	1,266	10,614
9	2,190	231	1,007	344	3,772
10	5,231	31	118	615	5,995
11	5,973	14	62	661	6,710
12	13,874	25	219	1,469	15,587
13	3,959	2,157	5,032	851	11,999
14	9,801	104	316	948	11,169
15	11,232	152	52	1,300	12,736
16	1,791	686	1,002	10,853	14,332
17	13,880	20	129	3,089	17,118
18	1,367	1,466	13,259	2,034	18,126
19	12,042	111	116	2,294	14,563
20	3,325	1,429	11,058	1,771	17,583
21	318	109	9,179	408	10,014
22	206	2,516	11,120	1,096	14,938
23	1,116	981	18,306	3,329	23,732
24	18	498	986	29,449	30,951
25	2,393	110	254	238	2,995
26	5,053	339	5,661	1,682	12,735
27	891	199	2,078	479	3,647
28	6	—	1,588	1,108	2,702
29	43	1,279	16,230	357	17,909
30	210	404	5,938	1,943	8,495
31	6,273	333	3,284	2,044	11,934
32	2,975	21	176	908	4,080
33	577	313	4,675	631	6,196
34	3,335	32	1	714	4,082
35	49	6	4	9,128	9,187
36	1,408	57	330	7,737	9,532
Total	131,293	16,087	145,445	108,071	400,896

PERCENTAGE RACIAL COMPOSITION, BY CENSUS TRACT, DURBAN: 1951 CENSUS

Census Tract No.	Percentages				
	Europeans	Coloureds	Indians	Africans	Total
1	11·78	3·00	74·30	10·92	100·00
2	69·54	4·52	3·46	22·48	100·00
3	69·09	0·27	1·32	29·32	100·00
4	9·14	3·58	58·88	28·40	100·00
5	1·59	4·88	88·32	5·21	100·00
6	2·32	4·89	77·33	15·46	100·00
7	1·28	0·60	35·20	62·92	100·00
8	60·76	5·84	13·45	19·95	100·00
9	51·55	5·63	23·99	18·83	100·00
10	74·36	0·55	1·75	23·34	100·00
11	67·13	0·53	0·92	31·42	100·00
12	74·96	0·45	1·24	23·35	100·00
13	31·22	17·16	39·92	11·70	100·00
14	73·03	0·95	2·44	23·58	100·00
15	78·39	1·16	0·37	20·08	100·00
16	12·07	4·67	6·80	76·46	100·00
17	79·14	0·13	0·75	19·98	100·00
18	7·16	7·77	69·87	15·20	100·00
19	80·60	0·80	0·78	17·82	100·00
20	17·81	7·84	59·61	14·74	100·00
21	3·13	1·10	90·81	4·96	100·00
22	1·35	16·55	73·55	8·55	100·00
23	4·56	4·07	75·07	16·30	100·00
24	0·05	1·50	2·93	95·52	100·00
25	70·03	3·43	7·78	18·76	100·00
26	36·80	2·59	41·61	19·00	100·00
27	23·39	5·36	54·82	16·43	100·00
28	0·22	—	58·75	41·03	100·00
29	0·24	7·13	90·26	2·37	100·00
30	2·43	4·72	68·99	23·86	100·00
31	49·29	2·71	25·87	22·13	100·00
32	62·19	0·50	3·72	33·59	100·00
33	9·23	5·04	74·95	10·78	100·00
34	70·03	0·84	0·10	29·03	100·00
35	0·50	0·06	0·06	99·38	100·00
36	14·43	0·60	3·39	81·58	100·00
Total	30·52	3·83	33·98	31·67	100·00

PERCENTAGE RACIAL COMPOSITION BY CENSUS TRACT (EXCLUDING NON-EUROPEAN DOMESTIC SERVANTS IN PRIVATE HOUSEHOLDS), DURBAN: 1951 CENSUS

Census Tract No.	Percentages				
	Europeans	Coloureds	Indians	Africans	Total
1	12·21	3·03	76·34	8·42	100·00
2	79·19	4·99	3·74	12·08	100·00
3	92·48	0·10	1·60	5·82	100·00
4	9·45	3·69	60·52	26·34	100·00
5	1·61	4·77	89·30	4·32	100·00
6	2·35	4·88	77·97	14·80	100·00
7	1·31	0·60	36·02	62·07	100·00
8	67·10	6·28	14·69	11·93	100·00
9	58·06	6·12	26·70	9·12	100·00
10	87·25	0·52	1·97	10·26	100·00
11	89·02	0·21	0·92	9·85	100·00
12	89·01	0·16	1·41	9·42	100·00
13	32·99	17·98	41·94	7·09	100·00
14	87·75	0·93	2·83	8·49	100·00
15	88·19	1·19	0·41	10·21	100·00
16	12·50	4·79	6·98	75·73	100·00
17	81·08	0·12	0·75	18·05	100·00
18	7·54	8·09	73·15	11·22	100·00
19	82·69	0·76	0·80	15·75	100·00
20	18·91	8·13	62·89	10·07	100·00
21	3·18	1·09	91·66	4·07	100·00
22	1·38	16·84	74·44	7·34	100·00
23	4·70	4·13	77·14	14·03	100·00
24	0·05	1·61	3·19	95·15	100·00
25	79·90	3·67	8·48	7·95	100·00
26	39·68	2·66	44·45	13·21	100·00
27	24·43	5·46	56·98	13·13	100·00
28	0·22	—	58·77	41·01	100·00
29	0·24	7·15	90·62	1·99	100·00
30	2·47	4·76	69·90	22·87	100·00
31	52·56	2·79	27·52	17·13	100·00
32	72·93	0·51	4·31	22·25	100·00
33	9·31	5·05	75·45	10·18	100·00
34	81·70	0·79	0·02	17·49	100·00
35	0·53	0·07	0·04	99·36	100·00
36	14·77	0·60	3·46	81·17	100·00
Total	32·75	4·01	36·28	26·96	100·00

CENSUS TRACTS IN EACH SOCIOGRAPHIC ZONE

SEA FRONT
3, 5, 17, 19, 32, 36

ALLUVIAL FLATS
7, 16, 18, 28, 29, 30, 33

SEAWARD TRANSITIONAL
8, 9, 10, 13, 15

BEREA RIDGE
11, 12, 14

INLAND TRANSITIONAL
2, 4, 20, 21, 22, 27, 31

PERIPHERAL
1, 6, 23, 24, 25, 26, 34, 35

APPENDIX C

Mean and *Per Capita* Income,
By Race and Census Tract,
Durban: 1951 Census

Q

ANNUAL MEAN AND *PER CAPITA* INCOME, BY RACE AND CENSUS TRACT, DURBAN: 1951 CENSUS

Census Tract No.	Europeans		Coloureds		Indians	
	Mean Income	*Per Capita Income*	*Mean Income*	*Per Capita Income*	*Mean Income*	*Per Capita Income*
	£	£	£	£	£	£
1	439·02	195·50	201·00	50·76	150·19	32·10
2	452·44	196·13	269·47	100·84	111·19	30·28
3	847·20	360·51	65·91	50·00	107·81	24·64
4	685·47	274·54	184·23	52·28	156·65	34·71
5	303·95	134·30	175·63	54·04	179·08	38·86
6	416·39	200·79	171·47	50·15	156·81	32·37
7	404·04	282·09	128·09	89·06	106·80	22·86
8	378·30	177·56	236·92	90·99	336·45	81·81
9	442·09	213·65	196·04	68·40	539·24	128·69
10	506·31	282·27	115·63	48·68	591·11	219·83
11	951·65	517·53	123·72	102·66	301·56	119·14
12	640·10	351·87	80·68	66·56	424·13	159·98
13	395·68	204·05	223·78	78·56	280·31	74·86
14	639·86	300·56	196·70	82·09	116·05	28·75
15	428·96	222·34	248·85	132·82	472·22	160·38
16	418·04	213·31	215·18	68·20	144·72	36·11
17	488·80	321·63	101·47	75·00	350·45	149·81
18	419·75	238·84	207·94	63·10	293·29	70·80
19	613·85	370·39	172·92	69·17	184·60	116·16
20	589·42	289·72	197·23	63·08	179·34	39·99
21	430·10	206·23	152·86	47·77	141·88	29·26
22	206·85	138·24	204·35	56·49	184·69	37·73
23	633·58	291·24	161·96	48·57	159·28	32·46
24	371·15	268·06	162·24	47·80	145·32	27·59
25	484·43	197·54	207·14	49·57	152·27	44·08
26	436·95	188·55	201·67	59·82	157·29	36·34
27	480·63	175·17	208·20	65·64	171·36	36·61
28	462·50	154·17	—	—	110·44	21·10
29	268·75	127·98	201·07	51·33	155·62	33·49
30	363·06	156·34	199·59	60·47	151·31	33·64
31	421·63	165·66	242·07	73·18	175·19	35·14
32	581·10	249·01	69·44	26·04	166·43	33·10
33	348·79	124·74	259·77	72·90	151·62	33·13
34	523·52	204·32	88·24	38·46	41·67	31·25
35	500·86	296·43	125·00	20·83	25·00	8·33
36	364·15	210·86	222·62	79·24	170·78	36·63
Total	552·06	282·74	201·20	64·34	182·85	40·02

INDEX

INDEX

DATE DUE